The TOP **60** since 1967

This book is available in quantity at special discounts for your group or organization. For further information, contact:

Triumph Books
542 South Dearborn Street
Suite 750
Chicago, Illinois 60605
(312) 939-3330
Fax: (312) 663-3557

Project editor: Jason Kay
Project consultant: Arnold Gosewich
Copy Editing: Sam McCaig
Proofreading: Suzanne Needs, Tom Donovan
Photo research: Matt Filion, Jamie Hodgson
Cover design: Matt Filion, Studio Andrée Robillard
Layout: Studio Andrée Robillard

Printed in Canada
© Transcontinental Books, 2007

ISBN 978-1-60078-084-4

The Hockey News

Ken Campbell and Adam Proteau

The TOP 60 since 1967

TRIUMPH
B O O K S

To Lucie, Connor and Lukas – my top three of the family expansion era.

– K.C.

For my mom and grandfather. And for tb, the first and the best.

– A.P.

Acknowledgements

The names Adam Proteau and Ken Campbell appear on the cover of this book, but the fact is that it was very much a collective effort, one that could not have come to fruition without contributions from many people.

The authors would like to thank:

Jason Kay, Editor of *The Hockey News*, for his foresight, diligence and his unwavering faith in us.

Sam McCaig, our top-notch project editor, who painstakingly went through the copy to make it readable and presentable.

Our other THN colleagues, Brian Costello, Mike Brophy, Ryan Dixon, Ryan Kennedy, Edward Fraser, Jamie Hodgson and Matt Filion, for their suggestions and support.

Gerald McGroarty, former publisher of THN, for his leadership and enthusiasm.

Jean Pare, publisher of this book, for his positive energy and support.

Arnold Gosewich, for providing valuable expertise and experience in what, to us, was the unknown world of book publishing.

Our panel of top 60 voters, Mike Brophy, Brian Burke, Jacques Demers, Jim Devellano, Kevin Paul Dupont, Jason Kay, Harry Neale, Jim Rutherford and Al Strachan, for their commitment and professionalism.

Nic Chabot of Fantasy Sports for compiling the post-expansion statistics.

The Hockey News' long and glorious history of columnists, editors and contributors, whose stellar work is often referenced in these pages.

Ken Campbell would like to thank Larry Brooks for providing him with much-needed Jaromir Jagr quotes, and also his family for putting up with his monopolizing of the computer on a nightly basis. Thanks to Gino Falzone for the advice.

Adam Proteau would like to thank Andrew Verner – whose goalie sketches and nose-bleeds at Maple Leaf Gardens helped cement his love for the game – and the rest of his degenerate friends, for helping him to laugh at life.

And finally, the players who participated in the project, for proving that they are not just great hockey players but great people as well.

Foreword

The sad reality is, I really don't remember much more than a few glimpses and flashes about my father as a Chicago Blackhawk. Might have something to do with the fact the Blackhawks never let kids inside the dressing room.

I do remember the old Chicago Stadium, though. When I was a youngster, I would sneak over to watch the visiting teams climb those legendary stairs to the ice. These men seemed like giants to me, and in the hockey world they were exactly that. Guys such as Gordie Howe, Jean Beliveau and Bobby Orr were awesome to me, even if I knew I was going home that night with my father, Bobby Hull, one of the greatest goal-scorers in NHL history.

It was a frantic time for the National Hockey League. Having doubled its size in one fell swoop in 1967–68, the league went from being a small pocket in the United States and Canada and extended its reach to California and the Midwest.

Even when I played in St. Louis, I got a sense of the history that NHL expansion brought to the Blues. They've never won the Stanley Cup, but just think of some of the players who have played there. It was a breeding ground for Scotty Bowman, who went on to become the greatest coach in NHL history. For a short time it was home to Jacques Plante, Doug Harvey, Glenn Hall, Al Arbour, Dickie Moore and Carl Brewer.

The NHL probably had no idea at the time that the Blues would become, with the exception of the past couple of seasons, one of the most solid franchises in the league.

The thing that struck me most about that era was the dignity of some of the league's biggest stars. Players such as my dad and Beliveau and Stan Mikita and Phil Esposito were true gentlemen. They played the game with ferociousness and did it at breakneck speed, but they did it as gentlemen who had an unabated respect for one another. In the 40 years that have elapsed since the league expanded, there's no doubt in my mind the erosion of respect has been one of the biggest and most detrimental things that has happened to the game.

My dad has been outspoken against the thuggery we've seen in the game – he even sat out for a short time during his World Hockey Association days in protest – and I feel the same way. I'm not talking about fighting, because I've been vocal in my support of it, but the lack of respect that players have for one another is at an all-time high and I, for one, find it embarrassing.

People often ask me what my dad might have accomplished if he had stayed in the NHL instead of moving to the WHA in 1972. Well, there's no doubt in my mind he would have become the NHL's all-time leading scorer. It doesn't surprise me he's on the list of the top 60 players of the expansion era, despite the fact he played just five NHL seasons – and part of a sixth at the end of his career – after expansion. Don't forget, he was coming off a 50-goal season in 1971–72 and was really in the prime of his career. I mean, he finished with 610 goals in the NHL, which left him fewer than 200 behind Howe at the time – and the way he was playing, he probably would have surpassed Howe's 801 within five or six years.

There's no doubt in my mind that he would have scored 900 goals in the NHL and might have even flirted with 1,000. As great a player as he was, the reverence for him would have been off the scales if he had stayed in the NHL. If the league could have found a way to harness the way Bobby Hull and Bobby Orr played the game, the NHL would've had it made.

I'll tell you another thing too. The Summit Series against the Soviets in 1972 would not have been nearly as close as it was if my father had played. He was faster than everyone else, he was stronger than everyone else and he shot the puck harder than everyone else. And I can also guarantee Bobby Clarke would not have gone out and broken Valeri Kharlamov's ankle, because my dad wouldn't have allowed it to happen. For him, it was always a gentleman's game.

And in my mind, there was no greater gentleman in the game than Wayne Gretzky, who, to the surprise of nobody, is No. 1 on the list. In many ways, I feel like I'm the most privileged player to ever play this game. I got to play for a short time with the greatest player ever, and I'm the son of one of the greatest ever. To have that in my blood and in my brain all these years has made the game wonderful for me.

To me, the big expansion in 1967 allowed a new generation to take the torch from the great players of the Original Six and keep the game going to where it is today. The 60 players on this list deserve to be celebrated, and I consider it a huge honor to be mentioned among them.

Enjoy.

– **Brett Hull**
May 2007

Table
of contents

THE TOP 60

Introduction

I n 1997, *The Hockey News* made a splash with our *The Top 50 NHL Players of All-Time* project, a credible initiative that ordered the NHL universe like never before. We leaned on 50 experts from all eras to cast ballots and help forge the "definitive" list.

So why upset that perfect alignment a decade later? Simply put, times have changed, and this is a different endeavor.

The Top 50 stretched back to the beginning of the NHL, all the way back to 1917, and relied heavily on historical and statistical information to bring players of bygone eras into perspective. It was executed thoughtfully and thoroughly.

But, as we approached the 60th anniversary of The Hockey News, we felt enough time had passed to revisit the list, update it and give it more of a modern flavor. And so *The Top 60 Since '67* was born.

We decided on 1967 for a few reasons. For starters, 40 years is a good sample size – not to mention a nice, round number. Many of us remember hockey in the 1970s, if not the late '60s; far fewer can put the 1930s, '40s and '50s into context. As such, it brings more of us into the debate.

Of course, 1967 was the year the NHL expanded from six to 12 teams, presenting another reason to use that season as our starting point.

And finally, much has happened in the past 10 years to impact on players' legacies. Steve Yzerman became a superhero/demi-god, Patrick Roy emerged as the best goalie ever, and Martin Brodeur started threatening all-time records, to cite a few examples.

With that in mind, we gathered 10 hockey experts, including yours truly, to set a new order for the past 40 years. The panelists are

– Brian Burke (GM of the Anaheim Ducks)

– Jacques Demers (Media personality and former NHL coach)

– Harry Neale (*Hockey Night in Canada* analyst and former NHL coach and GM)

– Jim Rutherford (Carolina Hurricanes GM and former NHL player)

– Kevin-Paul Dupont (Hall of Fame-honored hockey writer for the *Boston Globe*)

– Al Strachan (Hall of Fame-honored hockey writer)

– Mike Brophy (Senior Writer, *The Hockey News*)

– Ken Campbell (Senior Writer, *The Hockey News*, and co-author of the book)

– Adam Proteau (Online columnist, thehockeynews.com, and co-author of the book), and

– Jason Kay (Editor, *The Hockey News*).

We armed the panelists with stats and facts to use as guides when casting their ballots. Each voter was advised to consider only what players had done since 1967, making the pre-expansion contributions of stars such as Gordie Howe and Bobby Hull moot for this exercise. The voting results, and analyses of players' careers, are what you'll be reading about in the ensuing pages.

From this voter's perspective, it was a challenging and engaging assignment. The most mind-bending part wasn't comparing players of different decades but players of different positions. Dominik Hasek has won six Vezina Trophies as the league's best goalie and two Hart Trophies as MVP, while Joe Sakic has two major individual awards – the Hart and Conn Smythe – on his résumé. Does that automatically put Hasek ahead of Sakic?

And how do Stanley cups factor into the equation? Marcel Dionne, the fifth-highest scoring player ever, didn't get a championship sniff, but that doesn't make him a stiff. Would you put him ahead or behind Ron Francis, No. 4 all-time in points and a two-time Cup winner?

What about all-star nods? Luc Robitaille earned eight first- and second-team nominations, seven more than Yzerman. But Yzerman played in the Wayne Gretzky-Mario Lemieux era, a time when No. 3 was typically the best a center could hope for. Elite left-wingers such as Robitaille, on the other hand, were scarce.

And we won't even get into the Gretzky-Orr debate. Not yet. We'll leave that to the first couple of chapters.

We hope you enjoy the essays and arguments presented by our co-authors, Ken Campbell and Adam Proteau. We anticipate you'll disagree with them on occasion, shake your head, roll your eyes; but that's what makes hockey fans such a special breed. We're deeply passionate about the game we love, and most of us love a good tussle – at least verbal or mental, if not physical.

So let the debates begin…

– Jason Kay
Editor
The Hockey News

THE
TOP 60

1

Wayne Gretzky

The Greatest One

Wayne Gretzky's countless NHL records and dizzying array of distinctions are well known to casual and hardcore hockey fans alike. But you appreciate his genius all the more when you realize that every night he was going up against the very best players the opposing team had to offer.

"As fans, you'd see the Oilers versus the Bruins, or the Oilers versus the New York Islanders," said Gretzky, *The Hockey News'* top player of both the post- and pre-expansion eras. "But the reality was, I was facing the same small group of five guys every time we played them.

> **"But when [the Flames] moved to Calgary, we realized there was a dynasty in the making 180 miles up the road, and you'd start to have nightmares about [Wayne Gretzky] and the Oilers."**
>
> **– Cliff Fletcher**

"For example, when I played against the Islanders, I knew Denis Potvin would be on the ice every time. And although we played Calgary eight times in a season and then probably seven more times in the playoffs when I was an Oiler, out of those 15 games, I probably played against the same five or six guys every single shift.

"So you become very aware of individuals' tendencies after a while, and that's part of the game within the game that I loved playing so much."

We could fill up the rest of this book documenting all the high-water marks and milestones Gretzky achieved over his 20-year NHL career. Instead, let's do a quickie recap. He is the NHL's all-time leading goal-scorer (894) and point-getter (2,857). He won nine Hart trophies as the league's most valuable player, including eight straight (1980–87); two Conn Smythe trophies as playoff MVP (1985, 1988); 10 league scoring titles; five Lady Byng trophies for sportsmanship; and, of course, four Stanley Cup championships as captain of the Edmonton Oilers.

It was always about championships for the Brantford, Ont., native.

"Wayne wanted to be like Gordie Howe, wanted to be like [Guy] Lafleur, wanted to be like [Bryan] Trottier... guys who had won Stanley Cups," said Oilers teammate Paul Coffey. "When the Islanders beat us in '83, I remember him saying to me he'd never be remembered as a great player... like a Trottier, like a [Mike] Bossy... until he won a Stanley Cup. He was 100 percent right."

"Even from a young age, I was very aware of that," said Gretzky of his competitive streak. "When I was a kid going to tournaments, I can remember people saying, 'You guys had a great tournament, you came in second,' and I can remember my dad always preaching to me, 'Don't be comfortable with being second, that just doesn't cut it in professional sports. You need to win to be successful.'

"And when I first played [in the NHL] there were fewer teams, so I think the big-name or elite players hadn't accomplished anything until they had won a championship. There was always media pressure on individuals if they weren't champions. So whether it was Coffey or [Mark] Messier or [Grant] Fuhr, we were all extremely aware of that."

Former NHL GM Cliff Fletcher, who as the Flames GM had a front-row seat for the famous '80s-era battles of Alberta, quickly learned No. 99 could take over games like no one else.

"The second year the Oilers came into the league, [the Flames] were still in Atlanta," Fletcher said. "But when we moved to Calgary, we realized there was a dynasty in the making 180 miles up the road, and you'd start to have nightmares about him and the Oilers.

"Wayne's the greatest player I've seen lace on a pair of skates, as much for his competitive nature as anything else. Everybody always raved, and rightfully so, about his natural talent. But because of his demeanor and being soft-spoken, he fooled people sometimes about how competitive he really was.

"He was one of the most competitive players I've ever come across. You only realize that after you get to know him, but he just refused to lose. No lead was safe against a team he played on, particularly when he was in his prime with the Oilers."

Gretzky stayed in Edmonton until 1988, until the trade that shook the hockey world went down, and he was shipped to Los Angeles. However, he remains thankful he was a part of Alberta's finest on-ice moments.

"One of the things I was really fortunate about was I had a great sense of listening to what [coaches] Glen [Sather], John Muckler and Teddy Green were trying to preach to us about what would make us successful against each individual team and individual players," he said. "Sure, it was hard to leave Edmonton. That was my first NHL home, and some of the best hockey games I ever played were in Edmonton. But sometimes circumstances change whether you want them to or not, and it was time for me to go."

Gretzky continued to score at his trademark prolific pace with the Kings, but missed nearly half of the 1992–93 campaign with a wonky back. Unfortunately for Maple Leafs fans, he was healthy enough for the '93 post-season, and he proceeded to rob Toronto – and Fletcher, who was then in his finest year as the Leafs GM – of the Western Conference championship (and a Canadiens-Maple Leafs Stanley Cup final).

Wayne Gretzky Fast Facts

NHL career:	1979–99
Teams:	Edmonton, Los Angeles, St. Louis, NY Rangers
Post-expansion stats:	894 goals, 1,963 assists, 2,857 points in 1,487 games
Playoff stats:	122 goals, 260 assists, 382 points in 208 games
Individual awards:	
• Hart Trophy	('80, '81, '82, '83, '84, '85, '86, '87, '89)
• Art Ross Trophy	('81, '82, '83, '84, '85, '86, '87, '90, '91, '94)
• Lady Byng Trophy	('80, '91, '92, '94, '99)
• Pearson Award	('82, '83, '84, '85, '87)
• Conn Smythe Trophy	('85, '88)
First-team all-star berths:	8 ('81, '82, '83, '84, '85, '86, '87, '91)
Second-team all-star berths:	7 ('80, '88, '89, '90, '94, '97, '98)
Stanley cups:	4
Legacy:	The greatest to ever play the game.

"He was approaching the twilight of his career," Fletcher said. "In '93, we led that series three games to two, going back to LA for Game 6.

"I remember reading one of the local writers in a Los Angeles paper questioning whether Wayne still had the fire in his belly. I know [Leafs coach] Pat Burns and I looked at each other and said, 'Uh-oh.'

"Sure enough, Games 6 and 7 were two of the greatest games I ever saw him play. He was outstanding. He won the series for LA by himself."

Gretzky spent nearly eight seasons in Los Angeles and broke Howe's all-time goal and point records as a King before finishing his career with the Rangers (by way of St. Louis, where he played 18 games in 1995–96). It didn't matter where he played, though – Gretzky's office always was in the same part of the rink.

"My trademark was obviously playing from behind the net, and Glen was one of the first coaches that let us practise with the same five guys," Gretzky said. "Our line, [Esa] Tikkanen, myself and [Jari] Kurri, were always matched up with Paul Coffey and Charlie Huddy... they knew I'd be behind the net 95 percent of the time, so they'd get the puck behind the net and I could do my thing.

"And what probably made me was my ability to see the late man, the trailer. I could see Paul Coffey or Jari Kurri coming from what seemed like out of nowhere to somebody else, and hit them very, very late for an open shot."

His ultimate highlight, more than the Canada cups or any individual honor, was that first NHL championship.

"I don't think there's any feeling like it for any athlete," Gretzky said. "The first time you lift a championship trophy, it speaks volumes about your career and your teammates, and your commitment to winning. It's hard to win the Stanley Cup.

"Bryan Trottier had the greatest quote when he won it... He said how great it is to win the Cup, and you wish every player could experience that. But then he said, the reality is that's what makes it so special... so few players ever get the chance to get their name on the Stanley Cup."

Gretzky moved into management after he retired in 1999 and also was inducted into the Hall of Fame that same year. He loved remaining close to the game but admitted he'd have played forever if he was able to treat time like he did an opponent.

"Listen, when I played, I loved everything about it," Gretzky said. "It was a huge part of my life from the time I was two years old, and I know in my heart I did the best I could every night and prepared for every game.

"I wish we'd won more championships, but I'm proud of what I did in my career and can honestly say I have no second thoughts about anything I did until the day I retired."

– Adam Proteau

Bobby Orr

Peerless Defender

The season the NHL expanded from six to 12 teams was the same one in which Bobby Orr took control of the Norris Trophy and did not relinquish it for eight years. It was the season he began his trajectory from promising rookie to the best defenseman the game has ever seen.

It was also the beginning of the end of one of the greatest careers in NHL history.

By the time Orr hit the ice for his second NHL season in 1967–68, he had already endured one significant knee injury and had undergone the first of eight surgeries on the left knee that would ultimately betray both him and the hockey world. His second surgery came midway through the '67–68 season and limited him to just 46 games. But it wouldn't be long before Orr would redefine the defense position and put up the first of a mind-boggling six consecutive 100-point seasons.

When you listen to NHL scouts describe players today, some will mention the best ones in the same breath as Wayne Gretzky or Mario Lemieux, or at least they'll say the young man possesses some of Gretzky's or Lemieux's tendencies. But nobody ever compares anyone to Bobby Orr because there have been no comparable players. When he played, the gap between Orr and the rest of the league was enormous. And the gap between Orr and all other defensemen in the history of the game continues to be huge almost 30 years after he was forced to retire.

"In many ways, Orr was actually too good for the rest of us in the NHL," Philadelphia Flyers captain Bobby Clarke once said.

Orr certainly didn't see it that way. Still extremely reticent to talk about himself, Orr maintains there was no divine secret to his abilities. He is willing to concede that he possessed a sublime level of skill, but beyond that didn't see himself as anyone who deserved reverence or special treatment.

When asked whether he felt that enormous gap between him and the rest of the NHL, Orr said: "I never sensed anything like that. I was fulfilling a dream playing in the NHL, and that was what I thought about. All the records and all the nice comments are wonderful, but I was playing a game I loved. When I got to Boston, the guys treated me great, and they didn't have to. They were reading about this kid who was coming in, and they could have been really tough on me, but they weren't. They were great."

> **"In many ways, Orr was actually too good for the rest of us in the NHL."**
>
> **– Bobby Clarke**

For much of Orr's career, he watched people constantly elevate him and talk about how special he was, from teammates to opponents to media to fans. As uncomfortable as he is now with the notion, he was even more ill at ease with the accolades as a player. Although charitable to a fault – his former agent Alan Eagelson once referred to Orr as "a bleeding-heart do-gooder" – Orr was intensely private, even distant during his career. After a stint with the Chicago Blackhawks and the NHL's head office ended badly, Orr retreated to his privacy for more than a decade before resurfacing as a prominent player agent.

"I'm not colorful myself," said Orr in 1974. "I don't carouse around or get in trouble. I just go my own way, doing my own thing. I'm a private sort of person. I like my privacy. I'm on display every night anyway. I give all of myself in the games. That's the only me people need to know. What I do away from the rink is my business. Too much is made of me anyway. I'm a good player, but I'm far from perfect. I'm nothing special as a person."

Bobby Orr Fast Facts*

NHL career:	1966–79
Teams:	Boston, Chicago
Post-expansion stats:	257 goals, 617 assists, 874 points in 657 games
Playoff stats:	26 goals, 66 assists, 92 points in 74 games
Individual awards:	
• Norris Trophy	('68, '69, '70, '71, '72, '73, '74, '75)
• Hart Trophy	('70, '71, '72)
• Conn Smythe Trophy	('70, '72)
• Art Ross Trophy	('70, '75)
• Pearson Award	('75)
First-team all-star berths:	8 ('68, '69, '70, '71, '72, '73, '74, '75)
Second-team all-star berths:	0
Stanley Cups:	2
Legacy:	NHL's best-ever defenseman changed the way the game is played.

Fast Facts does not include any pre-expansion statistics or information.

Early in his career, he was even concerned that his style was influencing too many youngsters to be one-way players, but he defended his penchant for carrying the puck so much by saying, "I've been told I have to do it because it's best for the team."

So, often, Orr was able to do what was best for the team. Aside from being supremely skilled as a skater and offensive player, he also was tough enough to fight his own battles. And any time he carried the puck and got caught up ice after losing it, he had the speed and smarts to get back into position. That came from his days as a child playing on the Seguin River at the mouth of Georgian Bay in his hometown of Parry Sound, Ont., with no coaches trying to stifle his creativity. Because there was no glass off which to chip the puck, Orr became the best puck-carrying defenseman of all time. Most of his hockey as a youngster was played outdoors, and Orr remembers his team having to "wait our turn" to play at the indoor rink just like everyone else.

"My kind of defense was to handle the puck and not give it back," Orr said. "I couldn't play real defense because that wasn't my game. I didn't like sitting back, and I really didn't know how to sit back."

To suggest that Orr's opponents went into games thinking they could take advantage of his defensive play is ludicrous; they were far too worried about what he would do to them at the other end of the ice. Red Kelly, a former Norris Trophy defenseman himself, took note of Orr's defensive style when he coached the Pittsburgh Penguins in the early 1970s.

"My goodness, the young fellow is remarkable," said Kelly at the time. "I keep hearing about his weaknesses as a defenseman, but I've never been able to detect them myself. Why, look, he has the puck 95 per cent of the time he's on the ice. You can't get any better defense than that, can you?"

After 10 brilliant seasons and two Stanley cups with the Boston Bruins, a very bitter, very public divorce led to him signing with the Chicago Blackhawks. His knee was seriously damaged at the time, but Chicago owner Arthur Wirtz defended the $3-million deal by acknowledging it was a gamble and saying the Hawks were "putting our money on the nose of a thoroughbred." Orr played just 26 games over two seasons with Chicago, but was good enough on one knee to be named MVP of the 1976 Canada Cup.

"I was blessed with abilities to play a game I love," Orr said simply in describing his career. "And I played it with a passion."

– **Ken Campbell**

3

Mario Lemieux

The Savior

" The Rodney Dangerfield of hockey" (or, for that matter, of anything) is one of the worst clichés ever invented, so we won't tag Mario Lemieux with such a label.

Still, it's difficult to imagine a sporting legend who was given a rougher ride – in Lemieux's case, on the ice and off it – over the course of his illustrious career.

From the moment he arrived in the NHL, Lemieux was alleged to be doing something wrong. Whether it was his commitment to his country, his business dealings with the Pittsburgh Penguins or the hook-and-clutch style that held him back – and hurt his back – for years, Lemieux always was forced to defend himself.

Believe it or not, the following scenario actually took place: After he rewrote the QMJHL record books, after he finished a single season with 282 points and a 62-game point streak, after he almost single-handedly led the Laval Voisins to a Memorial Cup championship, and after the Pittsburgh Penguins drafted him first overall in 1984, Lemieux had to answer questions about his defense.

Which is like Tchaikovsky apologizing for being average at chess.

"I don't think Pittsburgh wants me to play defense," said Lemieux shortly after the draft. "What I think they want me to do is score goals and give a lot of points to the team."

Lemieux followed through on those expectations faster than anyone before him, scoring on his first NHL shot, on his first shift, in his first game for the Penguins. He put up 43 goals and 100 points in his rookie NHL season of 1984–85, and the accolades poured in right from the start.

He was the first and only rookie to be named MVP of the NHL all-star game and, at the end of the season, he was awarded the Calder Trophy as the NHL's top freshman. In his sophomore year, he amassed 93 assists and 141 points, second only to Wayne Gretzky in league scoring. His fellow NHLers voted him the Pearson Award recipient as the league's best player in the regular season.

But Lemieux was just getting started. In 1987–88, he broke Gretzky's seven-year grip on the scoring title and won his first of three Hart trophies. In 1988–89, he set personal bests in goals (85), assists (114) and points (199).

His brilliance translated well during international play. In the summer of 1987, Lemieux starred for Canada at the Canada Cup, setting a tournament record with 11 goals in nine games – including the deciding goal, set up by none other than Gretzky, that gave the Canadians the championship.

Lemieux was the perfect blend of size (six foot four, 235 pounds) and skill. Just ask one of the greatest goalies to play the game.

"Mario was the whole package," said Dominik Hasek. "Anytime he was on the ice, I told my teammates, 'Get to Mario.' I didn't care if somebody else was open, just as long as someone was covering him."

But because the Penguins didn't qualify for the post-season until 1988–89, questions about Lemieux continued. Many questioned his unwillingness to play for Canada in less-publicized international events such as the annual world championship.

> "Anytime he was on the ice, I told my teammates, 'Get to Mario.' I didn't care if somebody else was open, just as long as someone was covering him."
>
> – Dominik Hasek

Others questioned the Montreal native's passion for the game, mainly because he showed little in the way of emotion while on the ice. It wouldn't be long, though, before Lemieux was answering all of the naysayers the best way any player can – by hoisting the Stanley Cup.

"The first time I saw my name on the Cup after we won in 1991 was a big thrill," Lemieux told the Hall of Fame. "When you're a kid growing up in Canada, it's your dream to have your name on the Cup, especially for a kid like me, growing up in Montreal and watching those Canadiens teams win cups. Guy Lafleur was my idol. I wanted to be like him."

Lemieux also took home the Conn Smythe Trophy as playoff MVP in '91, validating his quiet leadership style. The truest test of his character was still to come, but it had nothing to do with pucks and sticks.

Midway through the 1992–93 campaign, almost a year after he led Pittsburgh to its second straight Cup – and captured his second straight Conn Smythe – Lemieux was diagnosed with cancer. He was also dealing with a recurring back injury made worse by opponents being draped all over him every night, and after playing sporadically in '93–94, Lemieux sat out the entire 1994–95 campaign to concentrate on his health.

No. 66 returned with a bang in 1995–96 – scoring 69 goals and 161 points, and winning his final Hart. He had 122 points the following season, after which he announced his retirement. The Hall of Fame waived the three-year waiting period for Lemieux, welcoming him as an honored member in 1997.

But his hockey battles were far from over. Especially off the ice.

Though the Penguins were successful on the ice in the 1990s, the business side of the team was hurting badly, and star players such as Lemieux were asked to defer their salaries to keep the team solvent. And when the Pens slid into bankruptcy, the biggest force in franchise history had to buy the team to keep it alive and attempt to recoup what he was owed as a player.

The cash-strapped Penguins were forced to deal away high-priced players during the initial period of Lemieux's ownership of the team, and crowds dwindled at the club's aging arena. So Lemieux took matters into his own talented hands and turned things around for his team once again.

In December of 2000, Lemieux ended his retirement, playing his first game on *Hockey Night in Canada* against the Toronto Maple Leafs. He notched an assist 33 seconds into the contest, finished the year with 76 points in 43 games and powered Pittsburgh to the Eastern Conference final. He hadn't lost a thing.

But he did have one more feat to accomplish – namely, winning a gold medal for his country at the Olympics. The night he arrived in Salt Lake City for the 2002 Winter Games, Lemieux told a reporter he had conserved his energy during the early part of the NHL season to prepare for his stint captaining Canada. "My priority this year was to play in the Olympics," he said. "That's why I haven't played too many [NHL] games, especially over the last couple of weeks."

Lemieux's remarks set off a firestorm of controversy, as some said he shook off his responsibilities with the Penguins for an exercise in nationalism. The same guy who was once ripped for not representing his nation in his early years was now getting blasted for doing so while his ailing hip would still allow it.

As always, none of the moaning mattered. Lemieux guided Canada to championship glory, potting two goals and six points in four games along the way. "I certainly took a lot of grief the last few weeks, but it was all worth it, just because of [the gold medal]," Lemieux said. "This was the chance of a lifetime, to play in the Olympics and do something great for your country."

When he retired for good in January of 2006, Lemieux had played 915 games over 17 seasons and finished with 690 goals, 1,033 assists and 1,723 points. Not to mention, he provided stable ownership for the Penguins when the franchise most needed it and in 2007 helped land a new arena for the team.

Admirable work for one of the greatest offensive minds in hockey history, even if the jealous and cynical rarely gave him a break.

"You can't please everybody, that's what I've found out in my career," Lemieux told *The Hockey News* in 2001. "It doesn't matter what I do, there are always going to be people that are happy and people that are [ticked] off. As long as the people that are close to me know the purpose and agree with my decision, that's all that matters."

— AP

Mario Lemieux Fast Facts

NHL career:	1984–97, 2001–06
Teams:	Pittsburgh
Post-expansion stats:	690 goals, 1,033 assists, 1,723 points in 915 games
Playoff stats:	76 goals, 96 assists, 172 points in 107 games
Individual awards:	
• Calder Trophy	('85)
• Pearson Award	('86, '88, '93, '96)
• Hart Trophy	('88, '93, '96)
• Art Ross Trophy	('88, '89, '92, '93, '96, '97)
• Conn Smythe Trophy	('91, '92)
• Masterton Trophy	('93)
First-team all-star berths:	5 ('88, '89, '93, '96, '97)
Second-team all-star berths:	4 ('86, '87, '92, '01)
Stanley Cups:	2
Legacy:	The game's most individually talented superstar saved hockey in Pittsburgh on and off the ice.

4

Mark Messier

The Messiah

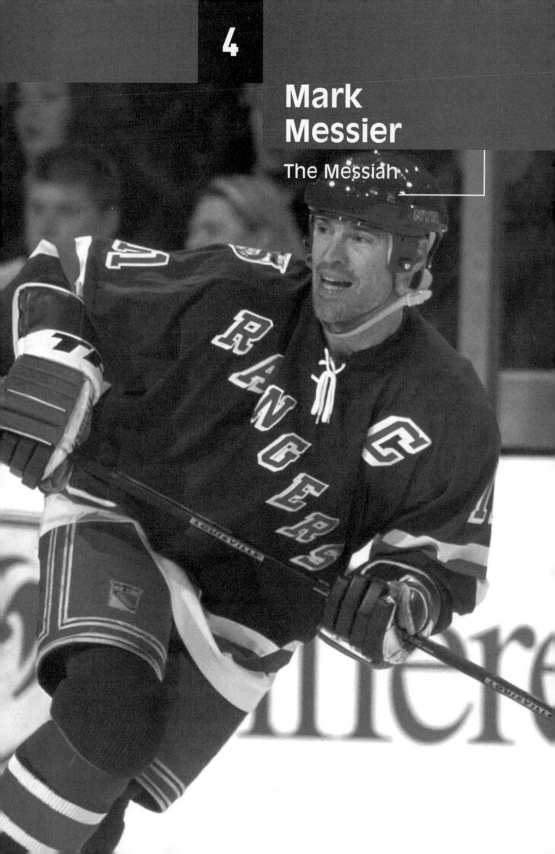

Conventional wisdom suggests some people are born to be leaders, while others are molded into leaders. Conventional wisdom be damned, though, when it comes to Mark Messier because he was a lot of both.

The born leader emerged from the bloodlines of Doug Messier, a university-educated, former tough-as-nails defenseman for the Portland Buckaroos who was instrumental in establishing a players' association for the Western Pro League in the 1960s.

The molded leader was made from the lessons he learned from his real father, his surrogate father, Glen Sather, as well as Wayne Gretzky and the players he had been skating with since he was 17 years old.

No matter whether the leader was born or made, or both, there is no disputing Messier was one of the most influential and powerful leadership forces the game has ever seen.

Oh yeah, and he could play a little bit too. Messier remains the only player in NHL history to be named a first-team all-star at two positions (left wing and center) and the only player to captain two different teams to Stanley Cup titles.

> **"I always tried to find out what motivated and drove people and how I might be able to help them unlock their untapped potential."**
>
> **– Mark Messier**

"I don't believe in born leaders," Messier said. "I just don't believe you become a good leader without having the right people around you teaching you how to be a leader."

How deep does it run? Well, the Mark Messier Leadership Award is as much about corporate sponsorship as it is about leadership, but the existence of an award that specific in his name gives you a pretty good idea.

But it wasn't always that way for Messier. In fact, one of the reasons Messier figures he was able to relate to all of his teammates was that he was not only a star player, but also someone who could speak on an equal level with fourth-liners and enforcers because he was one of them himself early in his career. In his first pro season as a 17-year-old in the World Hockey Association, he had one goal in 52 games. And it's not as though Messier came into professional hockey a sage veteran with all kinds of wisdom and leadership.

In fact, he was a young guy who made mistakes and errors in judgment just like everybody else. During his rookie NHL season in 1979–80, Messier earned a four-game stint in the minors for showing up at the wrong airport for a road trip to St. Louis. He was sometimes late for practise and occasionally didn't give everything he had.

Mark Messier Fast Facts

NHL career:	1979–2004
Teams:	Edmonton, NY Rangers, Vancouver
Post-expansion stats:	694 goals, 1,193 assists, 1,887 points in 1,756 games
Playoff stats:	109 goals, 186 assists, 295 points in 236 games
Individual awards:	
• **Conn Smythe Trophy**	('84)
• **Hart Trophy**	('90, '92)
• **Pearson Award**	('90, '92)
First-team all-star berths:	4 ('82, '83, '90, '92)
Second-team all-star berths:	1 ('84)
Stanley Cups:	6
Legacy:	Perhaps the best leader in the history of professional sports.

It prompted Sather to make an interesting observation about the young Mark Messier. "I think Mark could be an excellent pro once he learns to catch buses on time, be at the airport on time and discipline himself," said Sather in the early '80s. "He's got to learn hockey is the most important thing in life for now, and he must make sacrifices."

Consider the lesson learned. More than 25 years later, Messier still credits Sather with allowing him and his young teammates to learn their lessons rather than have them shoved down their throats.

"I think you need to allow 18-year-old kids to be 18-year-old kids," Messier said. "You can't cast them into these leadership roles before they're ready for it. You have to allow them to grow and mature as people, and part of doing that is allowing them to make the mistakes that 18-year-old kids make and letting them learn from those mistakes. As a coach, Glen was great for that. He demanded a lot from us, but he also believed in us, and he allowed us to be our age."

Slowly and progressively, Messier became the driving force behind the Edmonton Oilers. So mythical was his leadership aura that by the time he joined the New York Rangers in 1991, he was referred to as The Messiah. And like any good messiah, Messier directed his people to the promised land, leading the Rangers to the Cup in 1994 – and ending a 54-year drought.

And all those stories are true. In the days before cell phones became popular, Messier actually went out and bought one for each of his teammates, on the proviso that they used it to call him if they were ever in trouble, or for a taxi if they were in no shape to drive home. It's 100 percent true that Messier ordered all obstacles off the Rangers' training table so he could make direct eye contact with each player on the team.

But it wasn't all about pinning underachievers against the dressing room wall for Messier. Actually, he took a much more subtle approach.

"I always thought it was about developing interpersonal relationships," Messier said. "I always tried to find out what motivated and drove people and how I might be able to help them unlock their untapped potential. If you're constantly hurting guys and beating them down, it's not going to work. You have to get to a level of trust where you can be brutally honest with a guy and know that he won't think it's because you don't like him, and that you're actually doing it for their own good and the good of the team."

There are countless examples of Messier's take-charge attitude, but one of the best occurred at the 1987 Rendez-Vous series in Quebec City when Messier stood up in a room full of NHL superstars before the warmup.

"I don't think he had really spoken to anyone since arriving," Rod Langway remembered at the time. "Then in the room before the pre-game skate, he stood up and said, 'This is how we're going to do the pre-game skate.' He looked at Grant Fuhr and said, 'You're the starting goalie. Is that [warmup] good for you?' Fuhr just nodded. Then he looked around the room and said, 'Any objections?' I wasn't going to say anything. I was quaking in my skates."

Messier made opponents nervous too, both with his talents and belligerence. His elbows were legendary, and he was twice suspended for serious stick fouls. But it was his play and his ability to lead that will forge his way into the Hall of Fame.

"I always took it as a disappointment and a failure when we didn't win the Stanley Cup," Messier said. "It took a lot of heartache and heartbreak before we were successful, and with the exception of a couple of years, it worked out pretty well."

– KC

5

Patrick Roy

King of the Crease

Throughout his incredible NHL career, four-time Stanley Cup champion Patrick Roy always understood how misunderstood he might be. He just cared more about winning, that's all.

"My will to win was my greatest attribute on the ice," said Roy, one of the preeminent goaltenders in NHL history and the only player to win three Conn Smythe trophies. "I would do whatever it took. Some people would think you're arrogant for doing whatever you needed to, but for me the most important thing was winning.

"I didn't care what anybody's opinion was. What happened in that dressing room, that was the key."

Born and raised in Quebec City, Roy grew up cheering for the Nordiques before the arch-rival Montreal Canadiens made him their third-round pick (51st overall) in the 1984 draft. He joined the Habs in 1985–86, stepping in as an injury replacement for starter Steve Penney – and then stepping up as the youngest player ever to be named playoff MVP.

Not bad for someone whose 21st birthday was still ahead of him.

Patrick Roy Fast Facts

NHL career:	1985–2003
Teams:	Montreal, Colorado
Post-expansion stats:	551-315-151 record, 2.53 GAA, 66 shutouts in 1,029 games
Playoff stats:	151-94 record, 2.30 GAA, 23 shutouts in 247 games
Individual awards:	
• **Conn Smythe Trophy**	('86, '93, '01)
• **Jennings Trophy**	('87, '88, '89, '92, '01)
• **Vezina Trophy**	('89, '90, '92)
First-team all-star berths:	4 ('89, '90, '92, '02)
Second-team all-star berths:	2 ('88, '91)
Stanley Cups:	4
Legacy:	Retired as the NHL's all-time winningest goaltender.

"That first year was like a dream come true every time you went to the rink," said Roy, who shocked the NHL by going 15-5 with a 1.92 goals-against average during Montreal's post-season run in the spring of 1986. "It's funny, because I was on the plane that year, thinking, 'Wow, one year ago I was in school and math [class] was at 10:30.' "

Dubbed St. Patrick by devoted Canadiens fans, Roy quickly established himself as the team's most important player. In 1988–89, he went 33-5-6 to claim the first of three career Vezina Trophies.

"One of my goals right from the start was to be consistent," he said. "I didn't want to have an up-and-down career."

Central to Roy's consistency was a willingness to rest his body and mind during the off-season.

> "My will to win was my greatest attribute on the ice."
>
> – Patrick Roy

"Working out in the summer was not my favorite thing to do," Roy said. "I guess I felt that it was more important to have my mind fresh and to rest mentally. That way, I could start working with a clear focus when I arrived at camp."

Roy won his second straight Vezina in 1990, his third in 1992 and his second Stanley Cup in 1993. That second championship included an 11-game post-season winning streak, 10 consecutive overtime wins and his second Conn Smythe Trophy.

The 1993 Cup victory solidified Roy's already sizeable legend as a Canadien, but it did not guarantee his lifetime allegiance to the team. In an infamous incident at the Montreal Forum on Dec. 2, 1995, Montreal coach Mario Tremblay – with whom Roy did not have the best of relationships, to say the least – left him on the ice for nine goals in an 11-1 blowout loss to Detroit. Humiliated, Roy stormed off the ice when he was finally pulled midway through the second period, then made his way to team president Ronald Corey, who was seated immediately behind the Canadiens bench.

Roy told Corey he had played his last game in Montreal. Three days later, Roy was dealt to Colorado (for Mike Keane, Jocelyn Thibault and Andrei Kovalenko) in a trade that changed the destinies of Roy and the Avalanche for the better – and the fate of the Habs for the worse.

"It was a terrible time, no doubt about it," Roy said. "I really enjoyed my 10 years in Montreal, so it was very tough the way things ended. But it was fun bringing back hockey in Colorado. All the players really wanted to have success there, and we had a very good team right from the start."

Roy's revenge on Tremblay and the Canadiens was swift and supreme. He steamrolled through the 1996 post-season, sporting a sparkling 2.10 GAA and winning his third Cup and yet another playoff MVP award.

From that point on, Roy would never win fewer than 31 games in a single season, nor would his GAA rise above 2.39, until he retired in 2003. And when he won his final Stanley Cup in 2001, his 1.70 GAA in the playoffs was the lowest of his career.

He steadfastly refuses to accept all the credit.

"You need everyone, all your teammates on the ice, to come together and succeed to have that kind of a career," Roy said. "My teammates were precious to me, and I always believed in the team concept.

"I remember when we traded for Ray Bourque, someone said we'd have a hard time with all these stars on the same team. So it was a great challenge for every one of us to prove we could do it. And that's what we did."

When he retired, Roy held nearly every goaltending record worth owning. But that singular focus, the one that helped him win 551 games in the regular season and 151 more in the playoffs, kept his legacy out of his mind until the Hall of Fame came calling in 2006.

"To be honest, every time I was stepping in front of my net, it was not to make a place in the game... I wanted to help my team win," he said. "But when I went to the Hall of Fame, it helped me realize my place.

"Overall, I'm very happy to think I pushed my limits. Putting pressure on yourself is not necessarily a bad thing, but you have to back it up."

– AP

6

Steve Yzerman

Leading Man

Had Steve Yzerman's career unfolded the way he thought it would, the hockey world would have been robbed of one of its most creative and elegant players, not to mention a five-time 50-goal scorer.

Watching Yzerman over the last 10 years of his brilliant career – as a selfless team player who was defensively responsible and one of the greatest leaders the game has ever seen – it can be easy to forget he was once an offensive force, one whose sublime individual efforts made for spectacular goals, and plenty of them.

Even Yzerman himself has a hard time recalling that he was once that player. Never a big scorer in minor or junior hockey, Yzerman modeled himself after New York Islanders star Bryan Trottier, right down to wearing Trottier's No. 19.

"I don't even really know where that came from," said Yzerman of the offensive prowess early in his career. "The role I was definitely more comfortable in was that of the all-around player. I felt a lot better being that player, and really, that was the player I should have been all along."

> **"For me, there was always optimism, always improvement and always a light at the end of the tunnel."**
>
> **– Steve Yzerman**

Yzerman's talent level surprised almost everybody in hockey, particularly scouts who were watching the 1983 crop of draft-eligible players.

"Not only does this year's draft lack depth in terms of the number of good prospects available, but it may also lack quality at the top," said one scout in describing a draft that included Yzerman, Pat LaFontaine, Tom Barrasso, Cam Neely, Claude Lemieux, Bob Probert, Rick Tocchet and Dominik Hasek. "Not only is there no [Brian] Bellows this year, but there also is no [Gord] Kluzak, [Gary] Nylund or [Phil] Housley."

Other scouts were concerned whether Yzerman would be able to withstand the rigors of playing in the NHL, which is laughable now, after a career that spanned 1,453 games, many of them played in excruciating pain. One of the reasons Yzerman didn't stand out as much as he should have was that he played for the Peterborough Petes, who at that time were the New Jersey Devils of the OHL.

"Every night when I go to bed, I say a prayer and thank God for [Petes coach] Dick Todd," said Wings GM Jim Devellano early in Yzerman's career. "Thank God for Dick Todd and the fact he only used Steve Yzerman on every fourth shift and only sometimes on power plays."

Steve Yzerman Fast Facts

NHL career:	1983–2006
Teams:	Detroit
Post-expansion stats:	692 goals, 1,063 assists, 1,755 points in 1,514 games
Playoff stats:	70 goals, 115 assists, 185 points in 196 games
Individual awards:	
• Pearson Award	('89)
• Conn Smythe	('98)
• Selke Trophy	('00)
• Masterton Trophy	('03)
First-team all-star berths:	1 ('00)
Second-team all-star berths:	0
Stanley Cups:	3
Legacy:	Superstar leader rejected personal acclaim for team success.

Yzerman fell to fourth overall in the '83 draft, sandwiched between LaFontaine and Barrasso. By the time Yzerman arrived in Detroit for the 1983–84 season, the Wings were in a shambles. They had missed the playoffs in 14 of 16 seasons since the NHL expanded from six to 12 teams, and their Gordie Howe glory days were nothing more than a distant memory.

"We don't have enough players who can play in the NHL," said Devellano in 1982–83, the season prior to Yzerman's arrival. "We lack talent. This is basically an expansion team."

But from that despair emerged a three-pronged ray of hope. The first was Yzerman, who scored 39 goals in his rookie season playing on a line with Ron Duguay and John Ogrodnick. He led the Wings back into the playoffs, only to finish second to Barrasso in the voting for the Calder Trophy. The second was Devellano, one of the architects of the New York Islanders dynasty whose reputation in scouting circles was legendary. The third was Mike Illitch, a pizza baron who promised to provide the means to build a championship team in Detroit.

The Wings progressively built a solid franchise and sowed the seeds for a powerhouse at the 1989 draft, when they procured the likes of Mike Sillinger (11th overall), Bob Boughner (32nd), Nicklas Lidstrom (53rd), Sergei Fedorov (74th), Dallas Drake (116th) and Vladimir Konstantinov (221st) in what was one of the greatest single drafts in NHL history.

But the centerpiece was always Yzerman, both as an offensive wizard and later in his career, as a Selke Trophy winner. There were hard times, to be sure, from the early days with the Wings to several seasons of unfulfilled Stanley Cup expectations, but Yzerman persevered and was rewarded for it.

"It's funny, but things never seemed bleak to me," Yzerman said. "For me, there was always optimism, always improvement and always a light at the end of the tunnel. I never, ever thought we were going in the wrong direction."

Early in Yzerman's career, Devellano's five-year plan for a Stanley Cup saw the Wings advance to the 1987 and '88 conference finals against a far superior Edmonton Oilers team in the midst of a dynasty. And the Wings stumbled through the early part of the 1990s too, with a number of early exits and a stunning sweep at the hands of the New Jersey Devils in the 1995 Cup final. There was even talk that the Red Wings were considering trading Yzerman, that he couldn't lead the team to the ultimate prize, but they stuck by their captain and ultimately won three Cups with him.

In Yzerman's 14th NHL campaign, the Red Wings finally won the Cup – and they did it again the following season as Yzerman led the playoffs in scoring with 24 points and claimed the Conn Smythe Trophy as post-season MVP. It was one of a number of individual honors that Yzerman received late in his career, in part because he was no longer playing in the shadow of Wayne Gretzky and Mario Lemieux, but also because he had reinvented himself as a player.

"The hardest part about all of it was accepting that you're playing well and you're still an effective player, even though you go from 130 points one year down to 80 the next," Yzerman said. "All through that people were saying, 'What's happening to him? He's not the player he used to be.' Sometimes it takes a lot to convince yourself you're doing the right thing."

Yzerman was able to do that. And when he did, the Stanley cups and personal accolades soon followed.

– KC

7

Martin Brodeur

The Devils' Edge

Almost 15 years after he played his first game in the NHL, it sounds laughable, almost to the point of being outrageous. But the more you talk to Martin Brodeur, the more you realize he's being earnest when he says all he ever wanted to do was to be able to go back and tell his pals in the Montreal suburb of St-Leonard what it was like to be in The Show, even just for a little while.

"When I started my career, I wanted to just get one game in the NHL," Brodeur said. "After that it was just one win. That's just the way I approached it. I never took myself to be better than anybody else."

Well, Mr. Brodeur, history respectfully disagrees. Barring a career-ending injury, by the time Brodeur retires, he'll have more wins than any other goaltender in NHL history and will have easily broken Terry Sawchuk's record of 103 career shutouts, a mark once thought unassailable.

Martin Brodeur Fast Facts

NHL career:	1991–2007 (active)
Teams:	New Jersey
Post-expansion stats:	494-263-119 record, 2.20 GAA, 92 shutouts in 891 games
Playoff stats:	94-70 record, 1.93 GAA, 22 shutouts in 164 games
Individual awards:	
• **Calder Trophy**	('94)
• **Jennings Trophy**	('97, '98, '03, '04)
• **Vezina Trophy**	('03, '04, '07)
First-team all-star berths:	3 ('03, '04, '07)
Second-team all-star berths:	3 ('97, '98, '06)
Stanley Cups:	3
Legacy:	The backbone of New Jersey's defensive dynasty.

The reason Brodeur had that mindset early in his career was because there was little to suggest he was going to develop into one of the greatest puck-handling, clutch goalies the game has ever seen. In fact, some betting men might've predicted that Brodeur's career would more resemble that of his father, Denis, a good minor-pro and senior-league goaltender who won a bronze medal with the Kitchener-Waterloo Dutchmen at the 1956 Olympics in Cortina, Italy.

> "When I started my career, I wanted to just get one game in the NHL."
>
> – Martin Brodeur

Brodeur was seen as a very good, but not great goaltender coming out of junior in the QMJHL. He registered only four shutouts in 192 games for the St-Hyacinthe Laser, and his goals-against average in three seasons was never better than 3.39. In his final season of junior in 1991–92, Brodeur was beaten out for both top goaltender in the league and first-team all-star accolades by Jean-Francois Labbe. His first and only season in the AHL was quite ordinary. In fact, in that 1992–93 season, Felix Potvin, who was drafted 11 spots after Brodeur in 1990, was coming off a season in which he had been named the top goalie in the AHL and made a name for himself by backstopping the Maple Leafs to the conference final as a rookie.

In his draft year, Brodeur wasn't even projected as a first-round pick, and he was the consensus No. 2 goalie in the draft after Trevor Kidd.

"He's not very polished, but he has good physical tools," an NHL scout told THN's "Draft Preview" that year. "He's a rookie, and Kidd is in his second year. You can really see the difference a year makes. But in the long term, Brodeur might just rival Kidd in overall ability."

The New Jersey Devils, undeterred by the notion that Brodeur was a second-rounder, selected Brodeur with the second-last selection of a 21-pick first round. New Jersey's director of player personnel, David Conte, who has stacked the Devils and a number of other teams with his unparalleled drafting success, maintains Brodeur was the best pick he has ever made.

It certainly didn't take long for Brodeur to assert himself as an elite goaltender in the NHL. In his rookie season, only Mark Messier's tour-de-force semifinal performance – and perhaps a weakness on wraparounds – prevented him from leading the Devils to the Stanley Cup final. The next season, which was shortened by a lockout, culminated in his first of three Stanley cups to this point in his career. Only Brodeur and Sergei Brylin remained in 2006–07 from all three Devils championship teams.

For the longest time, however, Brodeur could not shake the reputation that much of his success came because the Devils were a defensive juggernaut coached by some of the most defense-minded men in league history. The numbers, to a certain extent, do bear that out. Among modern goaltenders, nobody has faced fewer shots than Brodeur. Through the midway point of the 2006–07 season, Brodeur had faced an average of 24.8 shots per game, almost a full four fewer than Dominik Hasek. Mike Richter, whose marvelous career was cut short by injury, faced 28.9 per game, Curtis Joseph 28.7, Grant Fuhr 28.1, Patrick Roy 27.6, Ron Hextall 26.9 and Ed Belfour 25.6.

But since save percentages began being recorded in the mid-1970s, only Hasek (.923) has recorded a better career mark than Brodeur's .913. And what many people fail to point out about the Devils is that while they don't allow a lot of scoring chances, they historically have not generated a lot of them either. Of his 92 shutouts entering 2007–08, 24 have been by 1-0 scores.

"We're not getting four or five goals, and they're always tight games, so every time you win you're always doing it under the gun," Brodeur said. "I just can't sit and relax."

Ironically, though, it was the 2002 Winter Games – 46 years after his father played – that cemented Brodeur's status as a goaltending icon. In backstopping Canada to its first Olympic gold medal in 50 years – to the day, no less – Brodeur feels that is where he escaped the reputation of being the beneficiary of a bunch of backcheckers.

"I think that was where I started winning my Vezinas and people started saying, 'Hey, maybe he is good,' " Brodeur said. "I think I needed to jump out of that Devils mold, and I think people doubt me less now. Even [in 2005–06] with all the changes, I was still the top guy in wins. But I don't think any goalie is going to have success with a bad team — I don't care how good you are. Look at what [Roberto] Luongo is doing [with the Vancouver Canucks]. Don't tell me he got better overnight. He's just playing with a better team. That's the bottom line, and after that you have to perform."

– KC

8

Ray Bourque

Quiet Genius

t is a measure of Ray Bourque's considerable hockey genius to hear him talk about the games within the game.

"A lot of times, the fun part of it was having your opponents do what you wanted them to do, in order to allow you to do other things," said the native of Montreal. "That was the chess match, offensively as well as defensively.

"A simple play is where you're protecting the front of your net and you've got your stick to one side. You know you're not covering anybody, and you're giving that guy a whole lane to pass the puck across the crease. And the minute he does, you know, and you move your stick and cut the pass off because that's what you wanted him to do.

"You're giving something and taking it away, and that was a thrill for me. You sold it and that's fun. In fact, sometimes it was comical."

There was nothing funny about the way Bourque competed during a storied career that ended in storybook fashion when he won a Stanley Cup with Colorado in 2001.

For more than two decades, Bourque was the scariest bear in the Boston Bruins' line-up. And it wasn't because he would overpower the opposition with bombast and brute force; rather, he would lure you into his lair at either end of the rink and maul you without making a sound.

> **"How I saw the game was probably my biggest strength."**
>
> **– Ray Bourque**

When he hung up his skates for good, Bourque had earned a Stanley Cup ring, five Norris trophies, a Calder Trophy, a Lester Patrick Trophy and a King Clancy Memorial Trophy. And his statistics, along with his statues, tell you everything you need to know about Bourque's impact on the game.

There are the records he holds for goals (410), assists (1,169) and points (1,579) by a blueliner. Then there's the fact he was named to the league's first or second all-star team in 19 of his 22 NHL seasons. Such numbers attest to a consistency that always was Bourque's primary concern.

"Numbers speak for themselves, but while you're playing, you know you're doing well but you don't want to acknowledge it," he said. "I just wasn't set on having one good day, or one good year. It was a matter of being at your best every day. Regardless of how you were doing in practise or game-wise, you wake up the next morning knowing you'll have to do it again and again."

Ray Bourque Fast Facts

NHL career:	1979–2001
Teams:	Boston, Colorado
Post-expansion stats:	410 goals, 1,169 assists, 1,579 points in 1,612 games
Playoff stats:	41 goals, 139 assists, 180 points in 214 games
Individual awards:	
• **Calder Trophy**	('80)
• **Norris Trophy**	('87, '88, '90, '94)
• **Clancy Memorial Trophy**	('92)
First-team all-star berths:	13 ('80, '82, '84, '85, '87, '88, '90, '91, '92, '93, '94, '96, '01)
Second-team all-star berths:	6 ('81, '83, '86, '89, '95, '99)
Stanley Cups:	1
Legacy:	The face of the Bruins for 20 years and then a champion Av.

Another of Bourque's talents was something that can't be taught – his near-unparalleled vision on the ice.

"How I saw the game was probably my biggest strength," he said. "I think special players have that. You know how to play the game, you know how to save energy and not run all over the ice. You know the anticipation. You see where the puck should or shouldn't go, or where it isn't supposed to go but it could anyway. It's having the courage to try things, and if it doesn't work one time, you make it work the next nine times.

"Even watching the game now, you still see it that way, but it's tough to teach it. It's tough to have other people see it the way you saw it, because you know it's a special gift that you have."

What didn't come naturally to Bourque was the in-your-face leadership style that many people expect out of someone captaining an Original Six squad. But during the 14 years he wore the *C* in Boston, Bourque earned the respect of his teammates and was widely acknowledged as one of hockey's elite quiet warriors.

"You lead without even trying to lead in some ways," he said. "To me, the best leaders are the ones who lead by example to start off with. How I practised and prepared without saying a word and showed the team what it takes to be successful… That came naturally to me.

"In other ways, when you've got to lead vocally and speak up and address things, some people might be naturals at it, while others grow into it. That was the case with me. It took me a little time to get comfortable, but I grew into it."

When Bourque went to Bruins management during the 1999–2000 season and asked to be dealt to a Cup contender, he was unsure whether he had another year of hockey left in him. After being shipped to Colorado and making it to Game 7 of the Western Conference final, he had his answer.

"It was very tough to leave Boston, but I really had some fun and found my game with the Avalanche," said Bourque, a Hall of Famer since 2004. "A lot of it was the mental part of it, being in a healthy situation. It was a rebirth in some ways for me. I really enjoyed the guys, the organization, and Denver was a really nice place to play.

"Your first year there, you're only there for a few months in a rent-a-player situation. So the next year it was fun to be there from day one. And having it mapped out the way we did, when Bob Hartley and the team talked about winning a Stanley Cup on the first day of training camp… was just an amazing experience."

Of Bourque's countless amazing experiences, Colorado's comeback from a 3-2 series deficit to beat New Jersey in the 2001 final stands out as particularly special.

"Game 7 was really a weird game," he said. "All along through the playoffs, when people asked me about playing for the Cup, I'd say we weren't playing for it until we'd won three games in the final and we were playing for that fourth win. And suddenly I was.

"Playing in that game, in a lot of ways it was one of the toughest games I've ever played in. We went up 3-0, and just trying to stay focused without letting your mind run and saying, 'I can't believe it, I think it's going to happen!' and just drifting off, is an incredible mental exercise.

"To have things work out the way they did, was just a great story, not only for me, but for hockey."

– AP

9

Nicklas Lidstrom

The Perfect Player

You'd be hard-pressed to find a more veteran observer of the NHL than Jim Devellano. And Detroit defenseman Nicklas Lidstrom would be harder-pressed to find a better tribute to his skills than the one paid to them by the former Red Wings GM.

"I've been in the league for 40 years, but I've also been following the NHL since 1956," said Devellano, currently the Wings' senior vice president. "The best defenseman and the best player I ever saw was Bobby Orr. But the second-best defenseman I have ever seen or been associated with is far and away Nicklas Lidstrom.

"I'll tell you why it's pretty special for a guy like me to say that: I'm the one who drafted Denis Potvin. And he was a pretty good player in his own right."

It wasn't difficult for Devellano to defend his ranking.

"Here's why I separate Lidstrom from Potvin, from Brad Park, from Chris Chelios, from Ray Bourque," he said. "[Five] Norris trophies. A Conn Smythe Trophy. Three Stanley cups. Five Presidents' trophies. A gold medalist for Sweden in the last Olympics.

"Most importantly, he's just very, very, very good at every aspect of the game. His skating is good. He handles the puck extremely well. He's got a terrific shot. He passes the puck tape-to-tape. He makes very, very few mistakes. And he's a horse. He has it all."

> **"He's just very, very, very good at every aspect of the game."**
>
> **– Jimmy Devellano**

As calm and humble off the ice as he is on it, Lidstrom defers to those around him when he hears his name included with those of the all-time greats.

"It's just a tremendous honor to be mentioned with those names," Lidstrom said. "I've been so fortunate to be in the right situation, with the right teammates, with the right organization. There's no way I could've accomplished the things I've accomplished without the help of a lot of people."

Neither the hockey world nor Lidstrom had grandiose expectations when he broke into the league in 1991 as a 21-year-old. However, two international tournaments against the game's best players gave him the confidence he needed to start his NHL career strongly.

"My first year, I just wanted to make the team," said Lidstrom, selected by the Wings in the third round [53rd overall] of the 1989 entry draft. "But I played for the national team at the world championship in 1991, and then I played in the Canada Cup that fall. Both of those international experiences were important for my development, and I felt comfortable right away in part because of those experiences.

Nicklas Lidstrom Fast Facts

NHL career:	1991–2007 (active)
Teams:	Detroit
Post-expansion stats:	202 goals, 666 assists, 868 points in 1,176 games
Playoff stats:	39 goals, 97 assists, 136 points in 192 games
Individual awards:	
• **Norris Trophy**	('01, '02, '03, '06, '07)
• **Conn Smythe Trophy**	('02)
First-team all-star berths:	8 ('98, '99, '00, '01, '02, '03, '06, '07)
Second-team all-star berths:	0
Stanley Cups:	3
Legacy:	Silky-smooth blueliner the only European-born player to win Conn Smythe.

"When you realize you can play and compete against the top players on an international squad, it makes you feel a lot better going into training camp with the Wings."

Lidstrom quickly established himself as an offensive force, putting up 49 assists and 60 points in his rookie campaign. But according to the native of Vasteras, Sweden, it was the defensive presence of a veteran partner that allowed him to excel.

"It helped a lot to play with Brad McCrimmon my first year," Lidstrom said. "I played pretty much every game with him as my partner that season. He was more of a stay-at-home defenseman, and that gave me the green light to go and join the rush. That really helped my rookie year."

It also helped that the Red Wings had so many skilled players around him. "At the very same time Nicklas was starting out, we were breaking in a guy by the name of Sergei Fedorov," Devellano said. "[Steve] Yzerman was still young, and we had another Russian rookie in Vladimir Konstantinov, so there wasn't much in the way of big expectations that were placed on Lidstrom. We thought he would be good, but he wound up being able to really play almost immediately, and he kept on getting better and better every year."

Interestingly, Lidstrom's all-around game blossomed when Paul Coffey – another blue-liner famous for his offensive talents – joined the Red Wings in 1994.

"After three or four years of playing with Paul, who was great at jumping into the rush as the fourth guy up there, I learned to stay back a little more and take more defensive responsibility," Lidstrom said. "Learning defense in the NHL comes with experience too. Figuring out how to play at both ends of the ice is a skill that doesn't come to you overnight."

Neither do stats like these: 1,176 NHL games played, 202 goals, 868 points. And, perhaps most impressive: Lidstrom has missed just 22 games in 15 seasons. That 98.2 percent average is the highest all-time percentage among players who have played 1,000 NHL games or more.

"And most of the games he missed weren't his choice," Devellano said. "Sometimes [coach] Scotty [Bowman] would sit him out the last one or two games before the play-offs began. So he's just been tremendously consistent in that regard."

For all of Lidstrom's honors, the biggest might be when the Wings named him Yzerman's successor as team captain in 2006–07, in the process making him the first European to ever wear the *C* in Detroit.

Aside from being a testament to Lidstrom's leadership abilities – let's remember, he remains the only European ever to win the Conn Smythe – Devellano said the captaincy is a reflection of management's belief the Swede's skills will remain formidable.

"We have to assume his skills will start to fade a little bit at some point because of his age," Devellano said. "So we say we'll cut his minutes. But somehow, you never wind up doing it, because whenever there's a penalty to be killed, No. 5 goes out there. Whenever you have a power play, No. 5 goes out there… When you know he can help you, having him sitting on the bench just doesn't make any sense."

Lidstrom is signed through the 2007–08 season, but Devellano believes he can play a lot longer.

"Nicklas could go on and play five more years for us," Devellano said. "And let's be clear: He is going to finish his career as a Red Wing. He ain't goin' to no other team. And when he retires, we're going to have a big ceremony for him in Detroit, just like the one we had for Stevie Yzerman.

"He'll deserve it every bit as much as Stevie did."

– AP

10

Phil Esposito

The Big Guy

As the radio color analyst for the Tampa Bay Lightning, Phil Esposito was crunching some statistics before a game when something suddenly dawned on him.

Esposito was looking at the stats for shots on goal when it finally hit him what he had accomplished when he took a mind-boggling 550 of them during the 1970–71 season.

"I just thought to myself, 'Holy s***, that's something like eight shots a game,'" Esposito said. "I couldn't believe it myself. I was a shooting machine that year."

Actually, the exact number is 7.05 shots per game, but you get the idea. In NHL history, nobody other than Esposito has ever shot the puck even 500 times in one season. The next highest total was posted by Paul Kariya with 429 in 1998–99, meaning the chasm between Esposito's total and the next highest player is more imposing than that of any NHL record-holder not named Gretzky.

Esposito earned the nickname The Garbageman during his 18-year career with the Chicago Blackhawks, Boston Bruins and New York Rangers, but he was so much more than that. Esposito had immeasurable leadership qualities, killed penalties, was outstanding on faceoffs, was a deceptively good skater and took shifts so long that the 6 foot one, 205-pounder simply wore down opposing checkers.

> "**Sometimes I think we were lucky to get the two cups that we did win, with the way we partied.**"
>
> **– Phil Esposito**

"I think Espo is underrated," said Bruins coach Harry Sinden after the 1970–71 season, in which Esposito established an NHL record with 76 goals. "As a matter of fact, I think he is the most underrated player in hockey. He should be rated a lot closer to Bobby Orr as the best player in the game."

He was twice named the game's best player, taking the Hart Trophy as MVP in 1969 and '74. He became the first player in league history to ever record 100 points and shattered the single-season goal total by 18 when he scored 76 times in 1971. Incredible feats, really, for a player who was cut by his local bantam team in Sault Ste. Marie, Ont., and struggled to make it as a pro with the Blackhawks. It was once written of Esposito that he showed "a disinclination to turn in the solid job of forechecking required of a center," and he often looked like a lazy underachiever in his three years with the Blackhawks despite scoring 20-plus goals each season.

"Phil isn't a natural skater," said then-Blackhawks GM Tommy Ivan, "so he's always been a step behind in every league."

Phil Esposito Fast Facts*

NHL career:	1963–81
Teams:	Chicago, Boston, NY Rangers
Post-expansion stats:	643 goals, 773 assists, 1,416 points in 1,047 games
Playoff stats:	57 goals, 72 assists, 129 points in 101 games
Individual awards:	
• Art Ross Trophy	('69, '71, '72, '73, '74)
• Hart Trophy	('69, '74)
• Pearson Award	('71, '74)
First-team all-star berths:	6 ('69, '70, '71, '72, '73, '74)
Second-team all-star berths:	2 ('68, '75)
Stanley Cups:	2
Legacy:	Cemented his legend status with a 76-goal season and a leading role in 1972 Summit Series.

Fast Facts does not include any pre-expansion statistics or information.

After Esposito went pointless in a first-round loss to the Toronto Maple Leafs in 1967, the Blackhawks dealt him, Ken Hodge and Fred Stanfield to the last-place Bruins in exchange for Pit Martin, Jack Norris and Gilles Marotte, a deal that is still regarded as one of the all-time greatest heists in NHL history. It was with the Bruins that Esposito became a true superstar, winning two Stanley cups and five scoring titles. All six of his first-team and both of his second-team all-star berths were earned while playing with the Bruins.

"I went to a team that was dead last and nobody was expecting crapola," said Esposito of his move to the Bruins.

It was there that Esposito and Orr set the foundation for a powerhouse. But there was always the sense that Esposito's teams could have done better. When he was with the Blackhawks, they were a dominant team with the likes of Bobby Hull, Stan Mikita, Ken Wharram and Doug Mohns, but simply could not close the deal in the playoffs. And while the Bruins did manage to win Cups in 1970 and 1972, there were more playoff failures than triumphs. And Esposito knows exactly why that happened.

"We should have probably won four straight Cups," he said. "But we got cocky and we weren't the most disciplined guys in the world. We just liked to party too much. Sometimes I think we were lucky to get the two Cups that we did win with the way we partied."

Perhaps Esposito's finest moment as a player and a leader came in the 1972 Summit Series between Canada and the Soviets. After first hinting he wouldn't play in the series, Esposito was named captain of the team and pulled it together through its darkest hours. The effect of Esposito's admonishment of Canada's hockey fans on national television after a 5-3 loss in Vancouver in Game 4 has been wildly overblown – the players didn't see it, and most didn't even know about it until after they returned home from Moscow – but Esposito was an enormous galvanizing force for the team in Europe. In fact, Bobby Clarke, who became one of the greatest captains of all time with the Philadelphia Flyers, said he patterned himself as a leader after Esposito's comportment with the Canadian team.

Esposito finished the series as the top scorer with seven goals and 13 points. Naturally, his 52 shots in the series were 20 more than the next frequent shooter, Alexander Maltsev of the Soviets.

"I knew somebody had to do it, and I knew it had to be me," Esposito said. "I knew there was no way we were going to lose that series, because I wasn't going to let that happen. I had just won the scoring championship, so what were they going to do to me? That's why I was so outspoken. At the first meeting in Toronto I stood up and asked Alan Eagleson, 'Where is all the money from this going?' and he couldn't answer me. That's when I should have run straight for the hills. He told us it was going into the pension fund. But whose pension fund? That's the question."

Esposito would win once more as part of the 1976 Canada Cup team, but the closest he ever got to another Stanley Cup was going to the final with the Rangers in 1979. Esposito was dealt to New York in 1975 – in another deal that shook the NHL – and was very good for the Blueshirts until midway through the 1980–81 season, when he simply realized he no longer had the desire to play anymore.

"When I realized what was happening," said Esposito at the time, "I was ashamed of myself."

By that time, a Hall of Fame career had been forged. Many observers claimed Esposito scored his goals from the crease, but he actually scored most of them from the hash marks.

"People ask me if I would like to be playing today, and I say, 'You bet your ass I would,' for two reasons," Esposito said. "One, nobody touches a guy in the slot now. Two, I'd be a $7-million or $8-million player."

– KC

11

Mike
Bossy

Gentleman Sniper

Conventional theory suggests that clutching and grabbing crept into the NHL quietly and gradually once the league began bloating in the mid-1990s and was running rampant for the first time by the early part of this century.

Mike Bossy doesn't accept that notion for a second. His brilliant career was snuffed out by back problems that were precipitated by a brand of hockey where star players were mugged and abused every bit as much – even more – than they were circa 2004, the last year of the "old" NHL. It was debilitating back pain that finally ended Bossy's career in 1987, when he was just 32 years old. But it was constant battles with the likes of Rick Zombo, Jan Erixon, Randy Cunneyworth and Doug Sulliman that really dealt the killing blow.

Perhaps the NHL should take notice. The league was robbed of Bossy's brilliance because it allowed far inferior players to nullify him with cross-checks and slashes – many of the same tactics being used against Sidney Crosby these days.

"I would challenge anybody to watch video of a game from the mid-1970s to the mid-1980s and not go through the first shift without seeing six or seven penalties that would be called today," Bossy said. "The hooking, the holding, the bullying was rampant."

> **" I guess as long as my arms are free, I can score a goal."**
>
> **– Mike Bossy**

Consider this: After watching Bossy score seven goals in the 1982 Stanley Cup final – to earn the Conn Smythe Trophy – in a dominant performance over the Vancouver Canucks, Dave "Tiger" Williams admitted, "I wanted to cut his head off during our first shift on the ice."

Bossy, an elegant and well-spoken man who now works in corporate affairs with the Islanders, vividly remembers what Williams said, remembering it was an accepted part of the hockey culture.

"I'm pretty sure if there was a quote in the paper today of someone saying they wanted to rip Sidney Crosby's head off, that guy would be suspended," Bossy said. "But that was just part of the way the game was played."

That's not the way Bossy played; his game was predicated on a magic scoring touch. Islanders GM Bill Torrey often remarked that when Bossy took a shot, it looked as though he didn't even touch the puck. Bossy seemed to appear out of nowhere with the puck on his stick and scored goals that looked almost impossible. And he often did it draped in defenders, prompting him to once say, "I guess as long as my arms are free, I can score a goal."

Mike Bossy Fast Facts

NHL career:	1977–87
Teams:	NY Islanders
Post-expansion stats:	573 goals, 553 assists, 1,126 points in 752 games
Playoff stats:	85 goals, 75 assists, 160 points in 129 games
Individual awards:	
• **Calder Trophy**	('78)
• **Conn Smythe Trophy**	('82)
• **Lady Byng Trophy**	('83, '84, '86)
First-team all-star berths:	5 ('81, '82, '83, '84, '86)
Second-team all-star berths:	3 ('78, '79, '85)
Stanley Cups:	4
Legacy:	Best pure goal-scorer of all time.

Bossy parlayed that remarkable talent into a career as one of the greatest pure goal-scorers in the history of the game. Coming off a junior career in which he scored more than 300 goals – and after inexplicably going 15th overall to the Islanders in the 1977 draft – Bossy said: "I've been a big goal-scorer all my life. I am confident I can help the Islanders, but sometimes things don't happen overnight. I hope everyone will be patient with me."

No need for that. Bossy went out and scored 53 goals as a rookie and still stands as the only player in NHL history to score 50 goals in nine consecutive seasons. When Bossy got the puck in "the wheelhouse," there were few in league history who were more dangerous or had a quicker release.

"I think a lot of that had to do with survival," Bossy said. "When I got to the NHL, I knew things would be a lot quicker than they were in junior, and I knew I would have to get the puck away quickly."

Among his 10 years in the NHL were five 60-goal campaigns and three consecutive post-seasons in which he scored a league-leading 17 goals. No player scored as many goals as Bossy did during his time in the NHL, and few were as prolific in the playoffs. With 85 goals in 129 playoff games, Bossy scored 0.66 goals per playoff game, second in modern history only to Mario Lemieux (0.71). The most impressive of those playoffs was the Conn Smythe performance in 1982, when he played the final with ligament damage in his left knee and the Canucks constantly mugging him.

"Scoring seven goals after being checked the way I was, I'm proud of myself," said Bossy after the series. "I'm damn proud I was able to perform in these circumstances."

In one game against the Detroit Red Wings in 1982, Bossy withstood an enormous amount of abuse and was knocked to the ice about 25 times in the game. The Detroit defense corps repeatedly pummeled him, and he couldn't go anywhere on the ice without being followed by Paul Woods, prompting Islanders coach Al Arbour to muse: "I think if Bossy had stopped and ordered a hamburger and a coffee, Woods would have done the same."

The back pain started at training camp in 1987 and was a constant problem all season. At one point, a two-hour bus ride from Long Island to Philadelphia left him aching worse than he ever had before. Not long after, Bossy realized his string of 50-goal seasons was about to end.

"It even hurts to say that," said Bossy, who finished his final NHL season with 38 goals in 63 games.

Pride, perhaps stubborn pride, often landed Bossy into arguments with teammates early in his career. He was a heavy smoker much of his career and always seemed on edge. Twenty years after retiring, though, he is much more relaxed, doing work for the Islanders and some radio in Montreal. He follows the game closely and watches the new NHL and generally likes what he sees. But through all the ebbs and flows, Bossy points out that nothing much changes.

"There are some good games and some bad games, good players and bad players," he said. "It has always been that way, and that's the way it always will be."

– KC

12

Jaromir Jagr

One-man European Invasion

Many truly great hockey players go their entire careers without ever earning a Stanley Cup ring. Jaromir Jagr had two of them before he had even mastered the English language or could legally buy a beer in the city in which he played.

It was certainly before he was old enough or experienced enough to fully appreciate the accomplishment. And, for the most part, it was before he became the mind-boggling individual talent who would win five NHL scoring titles and a Hart Trophy. For the 15 years following his two Cup wins with the Pittsburgh Penguins in 1991 and '92, Jagr compiled an impressive array of individual accomplishments. But, with the exception of a gold medal with the Czech Republic at the 1998 Olympics, he never came close to the team success he had as a teenager.

As Jagr reflected on his experiences as an older, wiser and mullet-less player, he was able to grasp the magnitude of what the Penguins had accomplished.

"I didn't understand what winning the Stanley Cup meant," said Jagr, a native of Kladno in the Czech Republic. "Remember, I came from a different culture and different hockey. I didn't appreciate the difficulty or what winning symbolizes. Later on I appreciated all of it, but not when I was 18."

It didn't take Jagr long to earn the nickname Mario Jr. when he joined the Penguins, and not only because it's an anagram of his own name. In his second NHL post-season, Jagr was an integral part of the Pens' success, stepping into the breach and supplying offense after an Adam Graves slash broke Mario Lemieux's hand in the second round of the playoffs. While not the best European player ever to play in the NHL, Jagr is the highest-scoring player either born or trained in Europe, making it official in 2006–07 when he surpassed Stan Mikita on the NHL's all-time scoring list.

> **"I didn't understand what winning the Stanley Cup meant."**
>
> **– Jaromir Jagr**

It is interesting to note that Jagr was taken fifth overall in the 1990 draft. While it would seem to be a cinch to suggest he should've gone No. 1, the revisionist draft order makes for an interesting debate when comparing Jagr's impact to that of Martin Brodeur, who was chosen 15 picks after Jagr. That Jagr was able to join a Penguins team loaded with talent and experience undoubtedly put him in a much more comfortable situation than he would've been had the woeful Quebec Nordiques drafted him first overall instead of Owen Nolan.

"It would have been more up and down," Jagr said. "But in that situation, I would've had to learn more from experience and from my mistakes. I would've been forced to be more of a leader at a younger age, and that would have been difficult because I hardly spoke English. The worst scenario is that I would have been an average player after my first five years."

That was certainly not the case, although Jagr did face an enormous adjustment as the first European to play for the Penguins. Bob Johnson, the deceased Hall of Fame hockey man who coached the Penguins in Jagr's first season, urged the Penguins to deal for Czech veteran Jiri Hrdina to help Jagr along.

"I was homesick all year," Jagr recalled. "There were times when I came close to going home."

Johnson was able to live with Jagr's defensive deficiencies and worked closely with him. Jagr still remembers Johnson as one of the best coaches he has ever had.

As brilliant as Jagr has been throughout his career, there have been a number of low points. At times, Jagr was portrayed as a brooding player whose effort level waned when he lost interest. During the 2006–07 season, he proclaimed to New York Rangers coach Tom Renney that he no longer wanted to participate in shootouts.

But nothing approached the misery he endured as a Washington Capital for two-plus seasons. Upon his arrival with the Caps prior to the 2001–02 season, he was hailed as the franchise savior, but he had two of the worst statistical seasons of his career while the team floundered.

When asked whether he gave up in Washington, Jagr responded, "No. They gave up on me."

He said they expected him to adjust to a rigid defensive system instead of building the team around his talents. "They took away my tools there," he said.

Jagr also signed an enormous long-term contract that nearly led the Capitals to financial ruin and created hard feelings among other players.

"Adam Oates was the captain and a great player," Jagr said. "He wanted a contract extension. They told him there was no money. Then they signed me for $81 million. How would that make you feel if you were Oatsie? I don't blame him for how he felt toward me."

Jagr was saved by a trade to the Rangers and the new NHL, both of which seemed to re-invigorate his career. In the first two full seasons after the lockout, only Joe Thornton had more points than the 219 amassed by Jagr.

"I'm very happy here," said Jagr of his move to the Rangers. "I don't ever want to play anywhere else."

– KC

Jaromir Jagr Fast Facts

NHL career:	1990–2007 (active)
Teams:	Pittsburgh, Washington, NY Rangers
Post-expansion stats:	621 goals, 907 assists, 1,528 points in 1,191 games
Playoff stats:	72 goals, 94 assists, 166 points in 159 games
Individual awards:	
• Art Ross Trophy	('95, '98, '99, '00, '01)
• Hart Trophy	('99)
• Pearson Award	('99, '00, '06)
First-team all-star berths:	7 ('95, '96, '98, '99, '00, '01, '06)
Second-team all-star berths:	1 ('97)
Stanley Cups:	2
Legacy:	The NHL's most dominant, talented European forward.

13

Guy Lafleur

A Flower with Flair

They rightfully called Guy Lafleur The Flower, for rarely was an on-ice bloom so beautiful as his.

In 17 NHL seasons, Lafleur brought a mixture of speed, sleekness, creativity and breathtaking skill. One of the most beloved Canadiens in history, he won five Stanley cups, three Art Ross trophies, two Hart trophies, three Lester Pearson awards and a Conn Smythe Trophy.

And he did so with a flair that made him a Habs legend.

"[Lafleur] is an artist on skates," wrote former THN scribe Bill Libby, "creating scoring plays the way a painter puts a vivid scene on a canvas with a brush... He sees where his opponents and teammates are and anticipates where they will be.

"He is a spectacular athlete in a spectacular sport and it is wonderful watching him work."

It was apparent from the beginning of Lafleur's junior career in Quebec that he would be a cut above the rest. He scored a mind-boggling 103 goals and 170 points in 1969–70 with the QMJHL's Quebec Remparts – and improved upon those totals the following season by netting 130 goals and 209 points, and capping it off with a Memorial Cup championship.

By the time he became NHL-eligible in 1971, Lafleur had created a huge buzz in the hockey world. The Canadiens, eager to continue the long tradition of French-Canadian superstars playing for Montreal, worked out a complex series of deals to all but ensure they would have the first pick in the entry draft.

> "A pass is a pass, but a pass to Lafleur is a goal."
>
> – Pierre Mondou

They chose Lafleur over fellow future Hall of Famer Marcel Dionne that year, and the young Quebecer who grew up idolizing Jean Beliveau suddenly had his fondest dream realized when he donned the *bleu, blanc et rouge*. He made the jump to the NHL right away, putting up 29 goals and 64 points in his rookie season, and thrived in Montreal's pressure-cooker hockey environment.

"I guess what I like best about playing for [the] Canadiens is that everybody is conscious of a championship feeling surrounding this team," he said at the time. "There's pride, good spirit. That's what's so nice about playing. Nobody lets down, everybody works."

Guy Lafleur Fast Facts

NHL career:	1971–91
Teams:	Montreal, NY Rangers, Quebec
Post-expansion stats:	560 goals, 793 assists, 1,353 points in 1,126 games
Playoff stats:	58 goals, 76 assists, 134 points in 128 games
Individual awards:	
• Art Ross Trophy	('76, '77, '78)
• Pearson Award	('76, '77, '78)
• Conn Smythe Trophy	('77)
• Hart Trophy	('77, '78)
First-team all-star berths:	6 ('75, '76, '77, '78, '79, '80)
Second-team all-star berths:	0
Stanley Cups:	5
Legacy:	The Flower used grace, skill to power Canadiens dynasty.

As well, Lafleur wasn't like some skilled players who did everything possible to avoid physical contact.

"Sometimes a hard check is good for you," he said. "It wakes you up, gets you in the game."

Lafleur's breakout offensive year came in 1974–75, when he netted 53 goals and 119 points in 70 games. He would reach the 50-goal, 100-point plateau for five more years afterward, making him the first NHLer in history to accomplish such a feat.

He set career highs in points (136) in 1976–77, goals (60) in '77–78, and assists (77) in '78–79, and starred for Team Canada at the 1976 and 1981 Canada Cup tournaments.

But at the height of his fame, Lafleur nearly lost his life.

On March 24, 1981, Lafleur fell asleep at the wheel and crashed his car into a highway signpost. The post nearly decapitated him; he was fortunate to escape only with a partially severed right earlobe that required plastic surgery.

Lafleur was shaken by the ordeal.

"I feel good… and very lucky," he told *The Hockey News* that April. "I think there was a message in what happened."

As the Canadiens' fortunes slumped in the early 1980s, so, too, did Lafleur's. His final 50-goal campaign was in 1979–80, and his overall numbers had dipped three straight seasons when he made a decision that shook Habs fans to the core.

Nineteen games into the 1984–85 season, Lafleur announced his retirement at the relatively young age of 33. A severe drop-off in his ice time and offensive output played a central role in the decision.

"I was in a slump, and I wasn't scoring much at the time," said Lafleur, who had just two goals and five points in 19 games that year. "After 13 years, I did not accept to be No. 2."

Calling his decision to retire "final," Lafleur managed to stay on the sidelines for three seasons and was inducted into the Hall of Fame in 1988. But the lure to come back proved too enticing, and he returned to active duty in 1988–89 – only he was wearing a New York Rangers jersey.

Hampered by an ankle injury, Lafleur tallied 18 goals and 45 points in his one year in Manhattan. The following season, he returned home to Quebec and played the final two years of his career with the Nordiques.

When he retired for good in 1991, Lafleur stood (and remains) as the Canadiens' all-time leader in assists (728) and points (1,246), despite playing significantly fewer games than the five Habs below him on the list.

In the end, Lafleur had no regrets and was pleased with his career.

"I'm proud of what I did in the past," he said. "I'm proud I played for the Canadiens, especially on five Stanley Cup winners."

– AP

14

Denis Potvin

Dynastic Defenseman

What is perhaps most impressive about Denis Potvin – other than the four Stanley Cup rings, three Norris trophies, Calder Trophy and the Hall of Fame plaque that bears his name – are the threads of familiarity that marked his entire professional career.

"I played five-and-a-half years of junior hockey with the [OHL's] Ottawa 67's, 15 years with the New York Islanders, and I'm in my 14th year with the Panthers," said Potvin, one of the game's greatest defensemen, who now serves as Florida's television analyst. "I value loyalty and I never want to complicate things."

Heck, even the infamous chants of "Potvin sucks!" have become a long-term staple at Islanders-Rangers games; even today, you can still count on hearing it at least once a game. (The chant began in the 1978–79 season after Potvin broke the ankle of Rangers forward Ulf Nilsson with a check that was, by most accounts, clean.)

"I've always done things in longevity, and I guess that chant is as loyal and as lasting as everything else in my life," said Potvin with a laugh. "It was not easy in the beginning to hear it, because it was mean and nasty, and there was a lot of true hatred that went along with it. But that chant is very much part of the lore of my career. And when you look back now and you understand its place in history, where we were and where the Rangers were, and fans were as passionate as I've ever seen about a rivalry. People compare what we had to the Yankees and Red Sox today, and how could you not be proud of being part of that?"

And how could Potvin not be proud of the way he played the game? After all, this is a guy who performed at a higher, better level than 99 percent of his peers, as evidenced by the fact he retired as the NHL's all-time leader in goals, assists and points by a defenseman. What's more, he did so with the spotlight and accompanying pressure following him from the beginning.

"I began dealing with pressures at a very young age," said Potvin, the Isles' first pick and No. 1 overall in the 1973 draft. "I started playing junior when I was 14 years old. The very next morning, the articles came out in the papers saying I was the next Bobby Orr. I just wanted to make the junior team.

"In many ways, the pressures were what I needed. When it was 10:30 at night and we had a game the next day, I had some pretty good offers to go to a party, have more fun. But for me, it was a responsibility to the next day. And I expected myself to be well prepared. It was like Eddie Westfall used to say, 'Why play the game if you're not thinking of winning?' "

> **"I only played hockey for one reason... I really loved it, and it was the best way to express myself."**
>
> **– Denis Potvin**

Potvin, who captained the Isles for eight seasons that included their dynasty years (1980–83), clearly excelled at winning. In his sophomore NHL campaign of 1974–75, the Islanders team – which had lost 60 games in its first year of existence just two seasons earlier – made it to the semifinal before losing to Philadelphia in Game 7.

The Isles returned to the semis in three of the next four seasons, but it wasn't until 1980, when they lost just six games in four playoff rounds, that they would win the first of four straight Stanley cups. That struggle to succeed, combined with management's willingness to keep the core components together, is credited by Potvin for the team's monumental achievements.

"It was truly a bond between all of us, and every guy had a role," said the native of Hull, Que. "Some guys had to be physical. [Mike] Bossy had to score. I had to play my game. [Bryan] Trottier had to play his game. Guys didn't want to disappoint one another, because that's who we played for. And for 10 years, we were a very, very good team, in part because we were allowed to be a team for a long period of time."

Potvin also played on a powerhouse of a team during his initial international experience.

"The 1976 Canada Cup in particular is very memorable to me," Potvin said. "I'd never had the chance to represent Canada in any format prior to that tournament. We didn't have the world junior back then. And it was a real emotional time in my life. I was 23, I'd just won the Norris Trophy, Bobby Orr had won it eight straight years prior to that, and we found ourselves on defense together in '76.

"I still hear Bobby Hull talk and say the greatest team he played on was that '76 team. And it was a real thrill to be there with a lot of my heroes. The entire experience was heartwarming."

In his work with the Panthers, Potvin has developed into one of the sport's most eloquent ambassadors. And when you hear him talk about his life among hockey's all-time greats, you quickly understand why.

"I wouldn't change my life and the choices I made for anything," he said. "I only played hockey for one reason... I really loved it, and it was the best way to express myself. Through the '70s and '80s, hockey was my life, and I didn't want to do anything else. And we were blessed to play at a time I truly believe had some of the greatest hockey ever."

– AP

Denis Potvin Fast Facts

NHL career:	1973–88
Teams:	NY Islanders
Post-expansion stats:	310 goals, 742 assists, 1,052 points in 1,060 games
Playoff stats:	56 goals, 108 assists, 164 points in 185 games
Individual awards:	
• Calder Trophy	('74)
• Norris Trophy	('76, '78, '79)
First-team all-star berths:	5 ('70, '72, '74, '76, '78)
Second-team all-star berths:	2 ('71, '73)
Stanley Cups:	4
Legacy:	Prototypical No. 1 defenseman could skate, score, pass and hit.

15

Bobby Clarke

A Philly Phenomenon

By the time he was 17 years old, Bobby Clarke had quit school and was working on the bull gang at the Hudson Bay Mining and Smelting Company in Flin Flon, Man. By day, he was thousands of feet under the ground, shoveling the residue left by the miners who were drilling the earth for copper and zinc. By night, he was a star for the Flin Flon Bombers.

From eight o'clock in the morning until noon, Clarke and his teammates would work in the mine, then spend the afternoon at hockey practise.

"And we'd get paid for a full shift," Clarke said. "I thought I was in heaven."

Clarke would have been content to live out his life in Flin Flon and work in the mines. The pay was good, the work steady, and every Friday night after their shift, the boys would go out for a couple of celebratory beers. That would have been Clarke's life had the Philadelphia Flyers not overlooked the fact he was a diabetic and chosen him 17th overall in the 1969 entry draft. (The Flyers' first pick that year, Bob Currier, never played a game in the NHL.)

"Of course I wanted to play hockey because I loved playing hockey," Clarke said. "But I wasn't running away from anything. There was no ulterior motive."

Clarke's medical condition almost kept him out of the NHL, but his determination, desire and sense of ruthlessness got him into the league and kept him there for 15 years. He was not the quintessential talent, to be sure, but to attribute all his success to his tenacity would not do justice to his underrated offensive talent and sublime understanding of the game. There are hordes of hockey players who would do anything to play just one shift in the NHL, but none of them is good enough to score more than

1,200 points, win two Stanley cups and make it into the Hall of Fame. In fact, Clarke was the first player – and remains one of only two – to win both the Hart Trophy as most valuable player and the Selke Trophy as the league's top defensive forward during the course of his career. (Sergei Fedorov is the other.)

Clarke has received a short shrift on the talent front, in part due to the fact he was the gap-toothed face of the Broad Street Bullies, who terrorized opponents en route to Stanley cups in 1974 and '75. Yes, Clarke was reckless with his stick, but he also used that stick to twice lead the league in assists and register three seasons of 100-plus points.

Clarke, though, did nothing to dispel that unflattering notion of him as a player. After scoring his 300th career goal in 1981, he held up the battered puck and said, "Look at this. It's an example of my stickhandling."

Clarke did come by his malevolence honestly, however. By the time Fred Shero was hired to coach the Flyers in 1971, Clarke already had been well schooled in the no-holds-barred style of hockey in Flin Flon under a junior coach by the name of Pat Ginnell.

> **"No player ever had more impact on his team, in hockey or all of sports."**
>
> **– Joe Watson**

"As it turned out, we played exactly the same style I played in junior, and Patty Ginnell had a huge influence on me," Clarke said. "The way we played was, hunt the puck and make someone pay. We played a style where we competed for 60 minutes at a high intensity, and there was a bit of ruthlessness to us."

A byproduct of all of that was a sense of courage, discipline and determination that is rarely seen in even the best athletes. Clarke's leadership qualities were legendary, prompting teammate Joe Watson to once say, "No player ever had more impact on his team, in hockey or all of sports."

Clarke, as a player and a person, was not overly complicated. Once, when the players' wives were asked to contribute their husbands' favorite recipes for the team program, Clarke's wife submitted "Hot Dog Surprise," a hot dog on a bun with mustard and relish. Never one to call team meetings or make others accountable, Clarke preferred to lead with his actions. At one point during the 1972–73 season, Clarke's blood count was so low because of his diabetes that he was told to stay away from practise for a few days. When he continued to show up, Shero had to threaten him with a fine to force him to stay home.

"In Philadelphia, a player can get $500 for signing autographs for an hour, two free cars, all the clothes he wants for nothing," said Clarke at the height of his career. "And all he has to do is work hard for two hours, 80 nights a year."

As Clarke moved into management with the Flyers, it was an attitude that he continued to espouse. Much like the teams for which he played, he simply took coming to work with the right attitude for granted.

"I always laugh when I hear people talk about teams and say, 'Geez, they work hard,'" Clarke said. "Isn't everybody supposed to be doing that? The way I was taught the game, if you can convince a team that hard work is normal, then it's not hard work."

Clarke made his mark both literally and figuratively on international hockey as well. His slash to the ankle of Soviet star Valery Kharlamov in the 1972 Summit Series has been well documented, but he was also a member of the team that won the 1976 Canada Cup. And he played for the NHL all-stars in the 1981 Challenge Cup and represented Canada at the world championship late in his career.

The 1976 Canada Cup united him with Montreal Canadiens coach Scotty Bowman, who once crossed swords with Clarke by calling him the dirtiest player in the NHL. But it was also Bowman who once paid Clarke a huge compliment by saying, "You take [Gilbert] Perreault. I'll take Clarke and I'll beat you."

– KC

Bobby Clarke Fast Facts

NHL career:	1969–84
Teams:	Philadelphia
Post-expansion stats:	358 goals, 852 assists, 1,210 points in 1,144 games
Playoff stats:	42 goals, 77 assists, 119 points in 136 games
Individual awards:	
• Masterton Trophy	('72)
• Hart Trophy	('73, '75, '76)
• Pearson Award	('73)
• Selke Trophy	('83)
First-team all-star berths:	2 ('75, '76)
Second-team all-star berths:	2 ('73, '74)
Stanley Cups:	2
Legacy:	Fearless captain of hockey's toughest Cup-winning team.

16

Paul Coffey

The Rover

Akey member of the Edmonton Oilers dynasty, Paul Coffey won four Stanley cups and three Norris trophies and remains the NHL's second-highest point-scoring defenseman.

But talk to the native of Malton, Ont., and you'll find he is just as proud of the professionalism he demonstrated over his 21-season career because, he said, it allowed him to retain his love of the game.

"The one thing I decided late in my career was that I was never going to leave this game negatively," said Coffey, a Hall of Fame member and Toronto-area businessman. "I've seen too many players who did. But the game was too great and gave me too much, so I was going to be positive no matter what and never take anything personally.

"That's why I still love the game today. I don't know how you can be bitter at this game."

Gifted with speed to spare and a first pass few could match, Coffey broke into the NHL in 1980–81. In attempting to prove his detractors wrong, he struggled in his early months as a rookie before accepting his role as a blueliner with the ability to make plays and put up points.

"One of the reasons I had a hard time was that I did something every young player shouldn't do: I read what people were saying about me in the papers," he said. "When you've got a player who can skate, pass the puck and shoot, people have to find something to pick you apart with, and with me, it was, 'The kid can't play defense.'

"So I went in there and tried to prove I could, and that wasn't why they drafted me. But once I got past that point, I played the way I was supposed to."

Paul Coffey Fast Facts

NHL career:	1980–2001
Teams:	Edmonton, Pittsburgh, Los Angeles, Detroit, Hartford, Philadelphia, Chicago, Carolina, Boston
Post-expansion stats:	396 goals, 1,135 assists, 1,531 points in 1,409 games
Playoff stats:	59 goals, 137 assists, 196 points in 194 games
Individual awards: • **Norris Trophy**	('85, '86, '95)
First-team all-star berths:	4 ('85, '86, '89, '95)
Second-team all-star berths:	4 ('82, '83, '84, '90)
Stanley Cups:	4
Legacy:	Defenseman's superb skating and offensive instincts set him apart.

When Coffey's sophomore NHL season ended, he had 60 assists and 89 points, the best totals of any blueliner in the league. Two years after that, he had 40 goals, 126 points and his first Cup. In 1984–85, he won another championship and was named the league's top defenseman. The next season, he added his second Norris Trophy.

Coffey credits the success he and the Oilers had to high expectations from both players and management.

"We pushed each other from within," said Coffey, who still stands as the highest-scoring defenseman in NHL playoff history, with 396 goals and 1,531 points in 1,409 games. "It's common knowledge we all enjoyed each other's company, it's common knowledge we had probably the best player to ever play the game, but we worked so hard. We didn't get a day off.

"[Coach-GM] Glen Sather, he was good, he was smart. He knew we were young, knew we were strong. He realized we were a bunch of stallions and we needed to be run hard. And he allowed us to have a personality on the ice."

Coffey's Oilers also benefited from being devoted students of the sport.

"To a man, every guy on that team respected the game," Coffey said. "Look at a guy like Denis Potvin. That's a guy I wanted to be like. He had championships.

"I couldn't wait to play the New York Islanders and the Montreal Canadiens, so I could watch Larry Robinson and Denis Potvin and try and learn from them. I never had a chance to play against Bobby Orr, but I would've just sat there and watched him and not wanted to play."

In 1987, Coffey became embroiled in a bitter contract dispute with Edmonton's ownership. He sat out the first part of the '87–88 campaign until the Oilers traded him to Pittsburgh as part of a seven-player deal.

> **"We were a bunch of stallions, and we needed to be run hard."**
>
> **– Paul Coffey**

Once settled in Steeltown, he did not disappoint. Coffey topped the 100-point plateau in each of his first two full seasons with the Penguins and helped the franchise to its first Cup in 1991.

Less than a year later, Coffey was on the move again, this time to Los Angeles. It marked the beginning of the end for him, the start of a period where he would play for seven different teams in a decade. But it also was a time in which he learned the true meaning of what it was to be a professional.

"As my dad had told me, I was a hired hand, that offensive defenseman teams were always looking for," said Coffey, who played for the Kings, Red Wings, Whalers, Flyers, Blackhawks, Hurricanes and Bruins before retiring in 2000. "I really thought, toward the end of my career when I was getting traded to all these teams, when I was a healthy scratch, that I was just being tested. I didn't know who was testing me, but somebody was.

"And I knew someone was always watching, so I had to be a professional. I remember playing with the Flyers, and I was a healthy scratch. Keith Acton was the assistant coach and he comes up to me and says, 'We've got to skate you.' And I said, 'Keith, tell me where to go and I'll go. I'm fine with it. Do your job, skate the hell out of me. If I'm not playing, I'm no different than a guy who's been in the league 10 minutes.'

"You're constantly being tested, and in those last three or four years, if I would've been a dick, that's the reputation that would've stuck. At the end of the day, your reputation is what it's all about, and it's the only thing you've really got."

– AP

17

Dominik Hasek

Unorthodox and Unbeatable

Growing up in Pardubice, Czechoslovakia, Dominik Hasek never imagined becoming one of the most dominant, decorated goaltenders in NHL history, not to mention playing at an elite level into his 40s. And now that he is, he can't imagine his life without the game.

"Oh, you know, I think hockey has been very good to me," said Hasek, a Stanley Cup champion with Detroit in 2001 and six-time Vezina Trophy recipient. "But when I was a kid, I didn't dream about the NHL. There were no satellites, no videos, nothing about the NHL in the newspaper. I didn't know anything about the league, other than there was hockey in Canada."

Instead, the man who would come to be known as The Dominator set his sights on suiting up for his country, and quickly gained international experience for the Czechoslovakians in the 1984 and '87 Canada Cup tournaments, as well as the 1988 Olympics.

The Chicago Blackhawks drafted Hasek 207th overall in 1983, but back then, the communist-era Iron Curtain made Eastern bloc Europeans all but impossible to bring over to North America. A thaw in international relations paved the way for Hasek to come to North America in 1990, but his NHL career began with a whimper as the backup to Ed Belfour for two seasons.

> **"The biggest accomplishments I've had are winning gold in the Olympics and winning a Stanley Cup... I have to put them next to each other."**
>
> **– Dominik Hasek**

However, Hasek's outlook improved immeasurably when Chicago dealt him to Buffalo in 1992. Suddenly, Hasek was afforded the opportunity that Belfour's presence had denied him in the Windy City. And, just as importantly, the Sabres gave their new No. 1 goalie the respect he never received in Chicago.

"In training camp in Buffalo, they asked me what number of jersey I wanted," Hasek said. "I thought, 'Oh, they mean it seriously,' because in the two years I was in Chicago, they never even asked me what number I wanted. They just gave me a jersey. So I thought, 'Maybe Buffalo is the right place for me.'"

For the better part of the next nine years, Buffalo was exactly the right place for Hasek and his much-noted, ultra-unorthodox style of play. In 1993–94, his second season with the Sabres, Hasek had a 30-20-6 record, a league-low 1.95 goals-against average and captured his first Vezina. In 1996–97 and '97–98, he went a combined 70-43-23, won two more Vezinas, and also claimed back-to-back Hart trophies, making him the

Dominik Hasek Fast Facts

NHL career:	1991–2007 (active)
Teams:	Chicago, Buffalo, Detroit, Ottawa
Post-expansion stats:	362-213-82 record, 2.21 GAA, 76 shutouts in 694 games
Playoff stats:	63-47 record, 1.99 GAA, 14 shutouts in 115 games
Individual awards:	
• **Vezina Trophy**	('94, '95, '97, '98, '99, '01)
• **Jennings Trophy**	('94, '01)
• **Hart Trophy**	('97, '98)
• **Pearson Award**	('97, '98)
First-team all-star berths:	6 ('94, '95, '97, '98, '99, '01)
Second-team all-star berths:	0
Stanley Cups:	1
Legacy:	Greatest European goalie in league history.

first netminder to win an MVP award since Jacques Plante in 1962 – and the only goalie ever to win two straight Harts.

Hasek's international career mirrored his successful trajectory in the NHL; its zenith came at the 1998 Olympics in Nagano, Japan. There, he led the Czech Republic to the young country's first hockey gold medal and was named the tournament's top goalie after eliminating heavily favored Team Canada in a semifinal shootout and allowing just two goals in the medal round.

For Hasek, that gold medal is treasured as much as anything he's done on the ice, before or since.

"The biggest accomplishments I've had are winning gold in the Olympics and winning a Stanley Cup… I have to put them next to each other," he said. "They're different accomplishments, for sure, as one is a short tournament and the other is a very, very long grind. But they are side by side as the best things I've been a part of in hockey."

It wasn't all accolades for Hasek during his Sabres days, however. In 1997, he feuded with coach Ted Nolan and the Buffalo media, who questioned the depth of his commitment to the team. And after a controversial call in the 1999 final cost the Sabres a chance at winning the Cup, Hasek's age, recurring groin injuries and a rebuilding organization resulted in him requesting to be traded in 2001.

"I felt like at that time, the ownership didn't want to improve the team, and if I wanted to win the Cup, I had to leave," he said. "In the end, I feel it was the right decision, and that's nothing against the Buffalo Sabres or the city. I have so many great memories in Buffalo. I just thought I didn't have a good chance to win the Cup there in 2002, and that's why I decided to move."

Hasek was dealt to Detroit prior to the 2001–02 campaign and did not disappoint, winning a career-high 41 games and going 16-7 with six shutouts and a 1.86 GAA in the playoffs. And, at age 37, he got to raise the Cup for the first time.

"It is an unbelievable feeling, winning the Cup," Hasek said. "You train for it, you hope you win it every year, but once you win it, it is a bigger feeling of accomplishment than you thought."

Hasek retired at the end of the '01–02 season, but his competitive juices continued to flow, and he returned to Detroit in 2003–04. Then, following the lockout, Hasek signed with Ottawa and played a strong half-season for the Senators before getting injured at the 2006 Olympics and missing the rest of the year.

The Red Wings took another chance on Hasek in 2006–07, signing the soon-to-be 42-year-old to a one-year deal. Father Time appeared to have no impact on him, as he went 38-11-6 with a 2.05 GAA.

His longevity can be explained, Hasek said, as a result of the fire within him.

"You must have talent to get to the NHL, but you must also have something inside," he said. "You must be a very, very hard competitor. If you aren't, you can't be a successful goalie."

– AP

18

Larry Robinson

A Rare Bird

For both his physical stature and his proficiency patrolling the blue line, Larry Robinson – who won six Stanley cups as a player and another as a coach – frequently was the center of attention during his NHL career.

But that wasn't always a good thing.

"When you're the size of a guy like Chris Pronger or myself, you stand out a lot more on the ice," said Robinson, who measured in at 6 foot 4 before he put on his skates. "And so everything you do and every mistake you make, especially when you play on defense, is magnified."

The magnifications also reveal Robinson's savvy on defense, which didn't grab the headlines his offensive contributions did, yet was nonetheless integral to the Canadiens' dominance in the late 1970s.

"I think the perspective of a defenseman changed over the years," Robinson said, "and with the exception of Rod Langway, most times back then people thought a defenseman wasn't regarded that highly unless he had a lot of points. But I took a lot of pride in the fact I was never a minus player throughout my career. Doing the job in your own end was important to me."

> **"That was the reputation I had as a player... don't wake me up, because I played better when I was angry."**
>
> **– Larry Robinson**

Born in 1951 and raised on a dairy farm in Winchester, Ont., Robinson spent his junior career with the Ontario Hockey Association's Kitchener Rangers before the Canadiens drafted him 20th overall in 1971. In his first season as a pro, he won the Calder Cup in the AHL with the Nova Scotia Voyageurs – and by the end of his sophomore season, Robinson was playing in the NHL as part of a Montreal team that went on to beat Chicago in the 1973 Stanley Cup final.

"A Calder Cup in your first year, a Stanley Cup in your second," Robinson said. "That's a pretty darned good way to start off your career."

Robinson's early success may have spoiled him, but he learned it didn't always come so easily.

"You go, 'Geez, that wasn't that hard,' " he said. "But when you play as long as I did, and when you coach after that, you understand how difficult it really is. You see someone like Ray Bourque, who won it in his last year [in 2001] when I was [coaching] in New Jersey.

Larry Robinson Fast Facts

NHL career:	1972–92
Teams:	Montreal, Los Angeles
Post-expansion stats:	208 goals, 750 assists, 958 points in 1,384 games
Playoff stats:	28 goals, 116 assists, 144 points in 227 games
Individual awards:	
• **Norris Trophy**	('77, '80)
• **Conn Smythe Trophy**	('78)
First-team all-star berths:	3 ('77, '79, '80)
Second-team all-star berths:	2 ('78, '81)
Stanley Cups:	6
Legacy:	Lanky defenseman starred for Canadiens' dynasty.

"I could've won two consecutive cups as a coach, but it helped seeing two guys like Bourque and Robbie Blake, two guys I admire a lot for the game they played, win their first."

Two other players Robinson admired as a child wound up as teammates during his greatest international experience playing for Team Canada.

"[The 1976 Canada Cup is] right up there with the Stanley cups," said Robinson, who also played for his country at the 1981 and '84 Canada Cup tournaments. "The Stanley cups are some of the greatest things I've ever done, because of the longevity of them. But '76 was very special for me. Bobby Hull was my boyhood idol growing up and he was my roommate in '76. And my defense partner in '76 was Bobby Orr. What more could a young farmer ask for?"

Robinson was the most all-around dangerous member of the Canadiens' Big Three defense trio, which included fellow Hall of Famers Serge Savard and Guy Lapointe. And though some players have shied away from the pressure that was part and parcel of playing in an NHL mecca such as Montreal, Robinson embraced it and excelled.

"I don't want to call it pressure, because I think that's something you put on yourself," said Robinson, who was awarded two Norris trophies and one Conn Smythe Trophy during his 20 years in the league. "But there was a sense you had to live up to the tradition of the Montreal Canadiens. It's what made great hockey players, or in some cases, destroyed other players.

"I honestly believe that if I'd played somewhere else, I might not have had the career I had. It wasn't just a game in Montreal. Even our practises… other people from other teams used to come in and watch us, because we practised like we played. Every day, you had to be at your best. You needed to have that drive. You needed to be pushed."

Robinson, affectionately known as Big Bird, had an easygoing nature that was perceived by some as a sign of weakness. However, almost everyone knew that – much like Dr. Bruce Banner of the *Incredible Hulk* series – you wouldn't like Robinson once you made him mad.

"That was the reputation I had as a player… don't wake me up, because I played better when I was angry," he said. "They said the same thing about my coaching career… I wouldn't make a good coach because I had too good of a personality. Well, I've got a Stanley Cup sitting on my mantle from being too nice. That's pretty good."

Robinson won his last Cup as a player with the Habs in 1986, then left the organization to finish out the last three seasons of his career with the Los Angeles Kings. And at least part of the success he's had as a coach – winning the Stanley Cup with New Jersey in 2000 – he credits to his experience as a player.

"Nobody can say, 'Well, what the hell did you ever win?' " Robinson said. "If you've had success, you've got that credibility.

"I wasn't one of those players who played off the seat of his pants. A lot of my game was natural, but a lot of my game I had to think through. That helped."

– AP

19

Bryan Trottier

Mr. Everything

Bryan Trottier was so unheralded as a junior player that any team in not one, but two professional leagues could have had him instead of the New York Islanders, and they all ignored him.

The year was 1974, and the NHL, so concerned about the rival World Hockey Association signing underage talent, agreed to pass a rule that teams could draft one 18-year-old prospect in the first two rounds of the draft. (The NHL also held the draft by conference call and in secret so WHA teams couldn't immediately begin poaching players from their protected lists.)

> "It's a lot tougher to play against [Trottier] than Wayne Gretzky."
>
> – Bobby Clarke

But Trottier, who hadn't even reached his 18th birthday at the time, went unselected in the first round before being claimed 22nd overall, the ninth underage player chosen in the draft. The Islanders wisely signed Trottier to a contract immediately and returned him to junior for another year. It was a decision that would provide the foundation for their dynasty.

Wayne Gretzky had an embarrassment of riches when it came to élan and grace, and Mario Lemieux may have been the most impressive physical talent to ever play the game, but Trottier will be remembered as the most versatile and one of the hardest-working players of his generation. Trottier could play in any situation and under any physical circumstances and still be the best player on the ice.

"It's a lot tougher to play against him than Wayne Gretzky," Flyers star Bobby Clarke once said. "That's because Bryan is more physical. He hits people. Hey, he'll run you as well as do everything else."

A testament to Trottier's impact on the game can be seen in one of the greatest leaders ever to play it. When he was growing up in suburban Ottawa, Steve Yzerman so idolized Trottier that he selected No. 19 and patterned his game after that of the Isles' superstar.

"Man, that's a pretty terrific compliment," Trottier said. "Steve Yzerman was much better than I was. He was a far better goal-scorer and had a lot better puck control."

Those who played against Trottier during the Islanders' dynasty years might beg to differ. Not only did he possess a wide array of talents, Trottier was a throwback in terms of industriousness. He grew up on a farm in Val Marie, Sask., and instead of getting involved in hyper-organized minor hockey, he honed his skills on the Frenchman River near his home. His work ethic came from the cattle ranch, where chores always took precedence over everything else.

Bryan Trottier Fast Facts

NHL career:	1975–94
Teams:	NY Islanders, Pittsburgh
Post-expansion stats:	524 goals, 901 assists, 1,425 points in 1,279 games
Playoff stats:	71 goals, 113 assists, 184 points in 221 games
Individual awards:	
• **Calder Trophy**	('76)
• **Art Ross Trophy**	('79)
• **Hart Trophy**	('79)
• **Conn Smythe Trophy**	('80)
• **Clancy Memorial Trophy**	('89)
First-team all-star berths:	2 ('78, '79)
Second-team all-star berths:	2 ('82, '84)
Stanley Cups:	6
Legacy:	Won four cups as Isles' star center, won two more as Pens' checking pivot.

"The only pressure you have on you is to bale hay in the summer," said Trottier early in his first season, one in which he broke Marcel Dionne's record for points by a rookie and won the Calder Trophy. "That's what I did to get ready for this season."

Trottier played 15 seasons for the Islanders, much of the time centering the team's Trio Grande Line between Clarke Gillies and Mike Bossy. In his first home game as an Islander, Trottier had a hat trick and five points. He was one of those few players whose work ethic and physical play matched his talent level.

"You can't teach his natural instincts," Islanders GM Bill Torrey once said of Trottier.

Trottier is one of only seven players – Lemieux, Gretzky, Joe Sakic, Mark Messier, Guy Lafleur and Bobby Orr are the others – to win both the Hart Trophy as MVP of the regular season and the Conn Smythe as MVP of the playoffs during their careers. He is the Islanders' all-time leader in assists and points and had a record 27-game playoff scoring streak that spanned three years. It's one of the few offensive records that Gretzky never even remotely approached – No. 99's longest post-season scoring streak, tied for second in league history behind Trottier, was 19 straight games.

Trottier's skills as an offensive player diminished in the late 1980s, and with Pat LaFontaine and Brent Sutter waiting for bigger roles, the Islanders bought out Trottier after the 1989–90 season. The Pittsburgh Penguins, looking for veteran leadership and penalty-killing, signed Trottier as a free agent, and he won two more Stanley cups with them. He won a seventh as an assistant coach with the Colorado Avalanche in 1996.

The times, however, were not all good for Trottier. A string of bad investments led to him declaring bankruptcy with debts of $9.7 million in the early 1990s, which brought on a deep clinical depression. It also forced him to come out of retirement for a year and delayed him having his number retired by the Islanders because he demanded to be compensated for his appearance at the event. (One hockey observer remembered seeing Trottier at an NHL all-star game, auctioning off much of his memorabilia and walking up and down the floor in front of bidders wearing sweaters he was trying to sell.)

Trottier was also a man who courted controversy. In 1984, he played for the US in the Canada Cup, claiming he wanted to give back to the country that had given him so much and was the birthplace of his wife. The son of a Cree-Chippewa Native, Trottier claimed he was a "North American citizen" and said his Indian Card allowed him to live in either country.

Late in his career, Trottier also wrote a piece in *The Hockey News* that eviscerated the league's officials. However, 20 years later, his words concerning clutching and grabbing have turned out to be prescient.

"The skilled players are just as skilled, but the less-skilled players are getting away with more because the officials have been less inclined to legislate against the garbage," Trottier wrote. "Stop adding more rules. Leave the game as it is. Just crack down. Call the rules as they are."

– KC

20

Joe
Sakic

Mr. Respect

Joe Sakic never will be considered a man of many words. But when your actions speak more to your on-ice brilliance than your mouth ever could, why waste the energy?

"I never really think of where I might fit in [hockey history]," said Sakic, a surefire Hall of Famer who began his career often being the lone shining light on some miserable Quebec Nordiques teams before evolving into a two-time Stanley Cup champion with the Colorado Avalanche.

"I'm just still having fun playing the game. That's really the only thing that matters to me at this stage. As long as I fit in, I'll be playing."

> **"The way you prepare, the way you stay at a certain level... that's what certain types of leaders show to the guys on the team. And that's what I was comfortable doing."**
>
> **– Joe Sakic**

Deeply affected by the tragic 1986 bus crash that killed four of his Swift Current Broncos teammates, Sakic first stepped onto the NHL scene with the Nords in 1988–89. A year earlier, he had won the WHL's scoring title and MVP award as well as the Canadian Hockey League's player-of-the-year honors, but many still believed him to be too small to make a significant impact in hockey's top league.

Sakic, a skinny 5 foot 11 kid when he was drafted, heard all the whispers, but refused to be defined by them. He would add 15 pounds of muscle to his frame over the course of his career and played in the NHL at 195 pounds.

"Going into the draft, you heard 'Not too big' and 'Not that fast,' " said Sakic, selected 15th overall by Quebec in 1987. "My leg strength did need to get better, so that was focused on for a while. I just knew that I could play in the [NHL], and I wanted and was willing to do whatever it took... all the little things that it took to win hockey games."

In his rookie campaign – on a last-place team that finished 27-46-7 – Sakic put up a more-than-respectable 23 goals and 62 points in 70 games. But it was in his sophomore season of 1989–90, in which he finished with 63 assists and 102 points, that Sakic truly emerged as a dangerous offensive threat and franchise player.

The inept Nordiques were slower to improve than Sakic and endured a six-year streak without a playoff appearance. That all changed in 1992–93 – not so coincidentally, the same season that management named the Burnaby, BC, native the team's captain.

Joe Sakic Fast Facts

NHL career:	1988–2007 (active)
Teams:	Quebec/Colorado
Post-expansion stats:	610 goals, 979 assists, 1,589 points in 1,276 games
Playoff stats:	82 goals, 96 assists, 178 points in 162 games
Individual awards:	
• **Conn Smythe Trophy**	('96)
• **Hart Trophy**	('01)
• **Lady Byng Trophy**	('01)
First-team all-star berths:	3 ('01, '02, '04)
Second-team all-star berths:	0
Stanley Cups:	2
Legacy:	Quiet, classy leader scored big goals and earned league-wide respect.

How could a mild-mannered guy such as Sakic take charge in the dressing room? By those same actions that rapidly were setting him apart from the rest of the league, that's how.

"There are different types of leaders in the NHL," he said. "The way you prepare, the way you stay at a certain level… that's what certain types of leaders show to the guys on the team. And that's what I was comfortable doing."

Sakic continued to hone his game wherever and whenever he could, including opportunities to play internationally. He was a crucial contributor on Canada's 1994 world championship team, which broke a 33-year-old gold-less streak at the tournament, and collected another gold medal – and was Canada's best player – at the 2002 Olympics in Salt Lake City.

"There's nothing like putting on your country's jersey," Sakic said. "You know everyone is watching, and the level of intensity goes up quite a bit. Those experiences probably helped me in the NHL, because I was learning there was another level of play."

In 1995–96, Sakic hit his stride, notching a career-best 120 points and hitting the 50-goal plateau. He also steered the franchise, in its initial season in Colorado after relocating from Quebec City, to its first-ever Stanley Cup.

"There's no describing the feeling you get the first time you lift the Cup above your head," said Sakic, who won the 1996 Conn Smythe Trophy after scoring 18 goals – including an NHL-record six game-winners – and 34 points in 22 playoff games. "We were building something special those last couple years in Quebec, and it would've been nice to win there, but that was a decision we couldn't control. I'm just thankful we won it."

In the summer of 1997, Sakic was a restricted free agent and signed a three-year, $21-million offer sheet with the New York Rangers. But he was able to stay in Colorado when the Avs matched the Blueshirts' offer (which included a $15-million signing bonus).

"At the time, either [the Rangers or Avalanche] would have been good," he said. "My childhood idol Wayne Gretzky was still there, and that would've been something if I could have played with him. But things turned out pretty well in Denver, I'd say. No regrets at all."

A three-time Olympian and 13-time participant in the NHL all-star game, Sakic won his second Cup with the Avs, as well as the Hart Trophy as league MVP, in 2001. Those dual honors make him only the fourth NHLer ever – Gretzky, Mark Messier and Bobby Clarke are the others – to captain their team to a Cup while winning the Hart in the same season.

At age 37, Sakic hadn't missed a beat in Denver. The franchise's all-time point leader (1,589 in 1,319 games) scored his 600th career NHL goal in 2006–07 and finished the season sixth overall in league scoring with his sixth 100-plus point total. And he's not finished yet.

"I still love playing," said Sakic, who signed to play his 19th season in 2007–08. "I'll have to stop one day. But not until my mind and body tell me it's time."

– AP

21

Jari
Kurri

The Finnish Finisher

Thomas Eriksson will officially go down in hockey history as an offensive defenseman who had a decent little career for the Philadelphia Flyers. But unofficially, he'll be remembered as the main reason why the Edmonton Oilers gambled in the 1980 draft on a Finnish right-winger named Jari Kurri.

At the time, NHL teams had no idea whether the European players they drafted would even bother to show up and play. Kurri's agent, Don Baizley, couldn't give Edmonton any guarantees that Kurri wouldn't stay in Finland for a couple more seasons. But Barry Fraser, the Oilers' progressive scouting director, who got burned the year before when they heard the same things about Eriksson, convinced GM Glen Sather to take Kurri 69th overall, in precisely the same spot they chose Glenn Anderson one year earlier and exactly 63 spots after Paul Coffey and 63 before Andy Moog.

You're probably familiar with how things turned out. The Oilers established themselves as one of the most dominant teams in the history of hockey, while Kurri was one of the best two-way players ever. Not just one of the best two-way European players, but one of the best, period.

The Oilers were too preoccupied winning almost every trophy known to man during the 1980s, but it does stand as one of the game's great injustices that Kurri never won a Selke Trophy. The closest he ever came was runner-up to Bobby Clarke in 1983.

"I was talking to Slats about that at the [sweater-raising] ceremony for Mark Messier in Edmonton," Kurri said. "And he said to me, 'That's the thing that pisses me off the most, that you didn't win the Frank Selke Trophy.' I don't know why, but maybe my numbers were too high."

Kurri has a point. Prior to Doug Gilmour taking the Selke in 1993, the trophy was reserved for the best shutdown forward in the league – and a forward who, until Gilmour won, had paltry offensive numbers. The league hadn't seen a defensive player quite like Kurri before, one who could shut down his opponent at one end and create offense at the other. Kurri scored at least 30 goals in each of the 10 seasons he played in Edmonton and scored 40-plus in seven straight seasons.

All of which made him one very prolific fire hydrant. That, of course, is in reference to Sather, who talked about Wayne Gretzky's previous right-winger, Blair MacDonald, by saying, "A fire hydrant could score 40 goals playing with Wayne Gretzky."

> "When Wayne [Gretzky] got traded, people were saying, 'Kurri is history. He can't play in this league anymore.'"
>
> – Jari Kurri

Kurri would later make Sather sheepish about that comment. He meshed with Gretzky because the two of them thought the game on the same level, and Kurri intuitively knew what Gretzky was about to do. More importantly, he was Gretzky's defensive conscience for eight seasons and allowed The Great One the freedom to create and be dangerous. Kurri also had the kind of deceptive speed from standing still to full stride that made it easy for him to get back into the play on both offense and defense.

Gretzky was almost always effusive in praising his right-winger and perhaps paid Kurri the ultimate compliment early in their careers when he quipped, "Hey, I'd like to see Jari get landed immigrant status so he could play for Canada in the Canada Cup."

For his part, Kurri did Gretzky's spade work without complaint. "Of course, someone must do it," he once said. "But I like it… no problem."

And make no mistake, Kurri hardly was riding on Gretzky's coattails. In the two seasons after Gretzky was traded to the Los Angeles Kings, Kurri posted seasons of 96 and 102 points. He scored 71 goals in 1984–85, then an NHL record for right-wingers, and remains third all-time in playoff goals (106) and points (233), behind Gretzky and Messier. In his last season in Edmonton, Kurri scored 10 goals and 25 points in the playoffs to help the Oilers claim their fifth Stanley Cup in seven years.

"When Wayne got traded, people were saying, 'Kurri is history. He can't play in this league anymore,' " Kurri said. "Definitely it was important for me to prove that to people, but I always knew as a player where I was and what I could do. But it wasn't always easy."

The post-Oiler years were not as kind to Kurri. A contract impasse with the Oilers – one of many the team had with players over the years – led him to play a year in Italy before a 1991 reunion with Gretzky in Los Angeles. After four-plus seasons as a King, Kurri was traded to the Rangers, and he also had stints in Anaheim and Colorado before capping his career with a bronze medal for Finland at the 1998 Olympics in Nagano, Japan.

As it should be, Kurri will always be remembered as an Oiler. It was in Edmonton that Kurri had his greatest successes and fondest memories of playing.

"I think you really have to give credit to Glen that he gave us the green light to get out there and enjoy it and do our stuff," Kurri said. "We were young, and we never had to worry about being benched or being sent to the minors. Nobody talks about that, but that's what a player needs when he's young."

– KC

Jari Kurri Fast Facts

NHL career:	1980–98
Teams:	Edmonton, Los Angeles, NY Rangers, Anaheim, Colorado
Post-expansion stats:	601 goals, 797 assists, 1,398 points in 1,251 games
Playoff stats:	106 goals, 127 assists, 233 points in 200 games
Individual awards: • Lady Byng Trophy	('85)
First-team all-star berths:	2 ('85, '87)
Second-team all-star berths:	3 ('84, '86, '89)
Stanley Cups:	5
Legacy:	Gretzky's right-hand man was first European-trained player to crack 600 goals and 1,000 points.

22

Brett Hull

One-timers and One-liners

O ne of the most famous photographs in hockey history is of an Adonis-like Bobby Hull as a young man, bare-chested and pitching hay at the family farm near Belleville, Ont.

At about the same age, Hull's fourth-born son was overweight, lazy and lacking direction in his life. That Brett Hull developed into The Golden Brett and not only matched, but eclipsed his famous father, is one of the most unlikely stories in the history of the game.

"He was always a kid who ran around with his nose snotty and his zipper undone," said the elder Hull about his son early in Brett's career. "And that's the way he played his first few years in hockey. He's never been a kid to sweat too much."

Whenever he was asked about what was passed down from his father, Brett Hull almost always replied "genetics" more than anything else. That's largely because it was hardly fatherly inspiration. Brett's parents had an unhappy relationship for much of his early life, and after their divorce when he was 13, Brett rarely saw his father until he began showing NHL potential while playing for the University of Minnesota-Duluth.

But there has always been that shot, that uncanny ability to get the puck off his stick like no other player. That, along with the obvious physical similarities, is where The Golden Jet and The Golden Brett most resembled one another.

They certainly didn't in their approach to the game. Bobby Hull oozed intensity and played every game with fierce determination. Brett, on the other hand, was one of the most loosely wound superstars in NHL history. As a teenager, he nearly quit the game, and he played recreational hockey for a year before starring with Jr. A's Penticton, (BC) Knights from 1982 to '84. He enjoyed playing hockey, but perhaps because of his name and legacy, never wanted the pressure of being driven by it. From minor hockey to the NHL, Brett possessed an uncanny ability to drive his coaches to distraction (see Hitchcock, Ken).

When he showed up in Penticton as an 18-year-old walk-on in 1982, he was 220 pounds, 20 more than his NHL weight, and almost none of it was muscle. But after scoring 105 goals and 193 points in 56 games in '83–84, Hull earned a scholarship at Minnesota-Duluth and was a sixth-round selection in the NHL entry draft by the Calgary Flames. He showed up the first day at Minnesota-Duluth wearing sandals, jeans and a sheepskin coat – and was so out of shape that teammates nicknamed him Pickle because they said he was round from top to bottom.

But after two very successful years at college, Hull, a Canadian-born dual citizen, accepted an offer to play for the US at the 1986 world championship and dazzled with seven goals and 11 points in 10 games. It wasn't an earth-shattering event at the time, but it set in motion one of the great careers in American hockey, highlighted by Hull's game-winning goal in the deciding game of the 1996 World Cup.

> "I took one of [Brett's] shots, and I'm still feeling it. And it was only a wrist shot."
>
> – Richard Brodeur

Prior to Hull's 1986–87 rookie pro season, Flames GM Cliff Fletcher said the organization was waiting to see whether he was for real. It wasn't a long wait. Hull scored 50 goals in 67 AHL games and, along with Joe Nieuwendyk, served notice he was ready for full-time NHL employment in the playoffs. Even though the Flames lost in the first round to the Vancouver Canucks, Hull had two goals and three points in four games.

"I don't know if the old man shot the puck that hard, because I never played against him," said Canucks goalie Richard Brodeur after the series. "But I took one of [Brett's] shots and I'm still feeling it. And it was only a wrist shot."

The Flames, believing they were on the cusp of a championship, shipped Hull and Steve Bozek to the St. Louis Blues in 1988 for Rob Ramage and Rick Wamsley in a deal that solidified Calgary's playoff lineup. But Fletcher, mindful of Hull's talent, first asked everyone in the organization whether they were comfortable trading a potential perennial 40-goal scorer for a shot at the Stanley Cup.

It was in St. Louis that Hull established himself as one of the greatest goal-scorers in the history of the game, recording three straight 70-goal seasons, including 86 in 1990–91, the third-highest single-season total in league history. But to brand Hull as a one-dimensional shooter with no other tangible attributes would be giving him the short shrift. Throughout his career, Hull played the game on a higher mental level than other players, and most of his goals were the result of him going to the right place on the ice and doing so without defenders being able to track him. He also was an under-rated playmaker and later turned out to be a useful defensive player too.

But there was always that propensity to stick it to the man. When Hull signed with the Dallas Stars as a free agent in 1998, he and Hitchcock were at loggerheads almost immediately. At one practise, after hearing Hitchcock preach constantly about defense – and not goals – Hull took the puck down the ice during one drill and dumped it into the corner. When an irate Hitchcock asked Hull what he was thinking, Hull simply said it had been made clear to him that goals were not important.

Hull finished his career with 741 of them, good for third on the all-time list and a place among the greatest scorers of all time.

– KC

Brett Hull Fast Facts

NHL career:	1986–2006
Teams:	Calgary, St. Louis, Dallas, Detroit, Phoenix
Post-expansion stats:	741 goals, 650 assists, 1,391 points in 1,269 games
Playoff stats:	103 goals, 87 assists, 190 points in 202 games
Individual awards:	
• Lady Byng Trophy	('90)
• Hart Trophy	('91)
• Pearson Award	('91)
First-team all-star berths:	3 ('90, '91, '92)
Second-team all-star berths:	0
Stanley Cups:	2
Legacy:	Nobody unleashed a slapshot, snap shot or wrist shot faster. (And he was pretty quick with the quips too.)

23

Marcel Dionne

The Forgotten Superstar

There they are in the Montreal Canadiens media guide looking so regal and elegant beside their embarrassment of riches in the form of multiple Stanley cups. The likes of Jean Beliveau, Henri Richard, Guy Lafleur, Yvan Cournoyer... all Canadiens goodwill ambassadors and all smiling and relaxed in their designer suits.

You can bet Lafleur never got his cuticles dirty from shaking hands after his playing career. Marcel Dionne, on the other hand, went from NHL superstar to Everyman. The day after he retired, he went to work, first opening a dry cleaning business, then, in one of the great ironies in hockey history, a plumbing enterprise where he would do much of the grunt work himself.

Think about it. One of the most prolific scorers in NHL history retired and became a plumber.

"I'm more involved with the bottom people than I am with the top people," Dionne said. "If you played for the Montreal Canadiens or the Toronto Maple Leafs, everything was given to you. Nothing was given to me. The 20th guy on those teams had a car. I never had a freakin' car. The only time I got a car was in junior because a guy in town helped me out."

> "When I played, I was a hungry, angry guy, and that's the way this kid [Sidney Crosby] plays."
>
> – Marcel Dionne

By the time Dionne had retired after an 18-year NHL career in 1989, he was pretty well equipped to go on his own. After all, he spent much of his career on the outside looking in. It was certainly that way in the playoffs. The teams for which Dionne played – the Detroit Red Wings, Los Angeles Kings and New York Rangers – had a combined .468 winning percentage and missed the post-season as often as they made it. In nine years in the playoffs, Dionne's teams made it beyond the first round just three times. The lone triumph on his résumé came at the Canada Cup in 1976.

Dionne was the most talented player in NHL history never to drink from the Stanley Cup. He was certainly the most dynamic one to never even come close. He played for moribund teams, to be sure, but Dionne must accept some of that responsibility himself. At one point in his career, he went four full playoffs with just one goal – and that went in off his leg. When he played his 1,000th NHL game, one of his Kings teammates congratulated him and then, only half-jokingly, asked how many of those games he actually helped his team win.

Marcel Dionne Fast Facts

NHL career:	1971–89
Teams:	Detroit, Los Angeles, NY Rangers
Post-expansion stats:	731 goals, 1,040 assists, 1,771 points in 1,348 games
Playoff stats:	21 goals, 24 assists, 45 points in 49 games
Individual awards:	
• **Lady Byng Trophy**	('75, '77)
• **Art Ross Trophy**	('80)
• **Pearson Award**	('79, '80)
First-team all-star berths:	2 ('77, '80)
Second-team all-star berths:	2 ('79, '81)
Stanley Cups:	0
Legacy:	The most talented, dynamic player to never win the Stanley Cup.

There was no shortage of Dionne critics throughout his career, and he gave them much fodder. When Dionne was just 17 years old, he spurned his native Quebec to play junior for the St. Catharines Blackhawks of the Ontario Hockey Association. As well, he crossed swords with management many times early in his career. The Red Wings, who drafted him second overall after the Canadiens took Lafleur in 1971, suspended him several times in the four years he played there.

Early in the 1972–73 season, Dionne bolted from practise and then didn't show up for a game against the Vancouver Canucks. One year later, Wings coach Ted Garvin suspended him for lackluster play. "He won't even say what is bothering him, why he isn't producing," said Garvin at the time. "I just don't understand him."

Dionne became the first high-profile NHL player to sign with another team when the Los Angeles Kings gave him $1.5 million over five years to be their franchise player in 1975, just days after Kings owner Jerry Buss announced that he had acquired Kareem Abdul-Jabbar for the Lakers. It spoke volumes that Kings coach Bob Pulford did not attend the news conference for Dionne's signing.

And while Abdul-Jabbar went on to win five NBA championships in Los Angeles, Dionne's teams floundered every bit as badly as the Red Wings.

Dionne threatened to retire or bolt to the World Hockey Association several times during his tenure with the Kings. One of those times was in 1980 when, at the age of 28, Dionne blasted both the team management and players and said he was considering leaving the game.

"You can't win games without talent, and I'm one of the few guys who has it," said Dionne at the time. "It's up to the general manager. If he can't judge talent, I hope he can judge character, because that's something else we haven't got. I'm tired of busting my butt and having these fat cats live off me."

After a brawl-filled game against the Philadelphia Flyers in 1974, Dionne threatened to retire, saying, "What's the league waiting for, somebody to die out there?"

But there was no disputing Dionne's remarkable talent. He retired with stats far superior to Lafleur's and ranks fifth on the NHL's all-time scoring list. When he watches games today, he looks at Sidney Crosby and sees a lot of himself in the budding superstar.

"Oh yeah, big-time," said Dionne when asked whether Crosby reminds him of himself. "When I played, I was a hungry, angry guy and that's the way this kid plays. You want to take that puck away from me and somebody has to pay the price."

Aside from not winning the Stanley Cup, Dionne said his biggest regret was not playing his career in a market that was passionate about hockey.

"The biggest disappointment I had is the people of Canada never had the opportunity to see me play," Dionne said. "You had *Hockey Night in Canada* and everyone across the country saw Guy Lafleur all the time. Me, it was five games a year on TV in LA. When I came in, we didn't have cable TV. I watch the highlights now and I hear people say, 'Oh, look at this goal, look at that goal.' I had about a freakin' hundred like that."

They just didn't come in the spring. In 1981, the Kings finished fourth overall in the league, but lost a best-of-five first-round playoff series to the upstart Rangers, who were the 13th seed, in four games. Dionne, who had a goal and four points against the Rangers, uttered after the series what might have been the epitaph for his career.

"I could have been a hero," he said.

– **KC**

24

Peter Forsberg

Tour de Fors

Peter Forsberg Fast Facts

NHL career:	1995–2007 (active)
Teams:	Quebec/Colorado, Philadelphia, Nashville
Post-expansion stats:	248 goals, 623 assists, 871 points in 697 games
Playoff stats:	63 goals, 103 assists, 166 points in 144 games
Individual awards:	
• Calder Trophy	('95)
• Art Ross Trophy	('03)
• Hart Trophy	('03)
First-team all-star berths:	3 ('98, '99, '03)
Second-team all-star berths:	0
Stanley Cups:	2
Legacy:	Dominant performer overcame significant injuries to lead Avs to promised land.

I n 1992, a brilliant, if relatively unknown prospect from Sweden was one of six players the Flyers dealt to Quebec in what was long known as the Eric Lindros trade.

More than 15 years later, the transaction ought to be known as the Peter Forsberg trade. And if the Flyers could do it all over again knowing what they know now, it's quite likely Lindros never would've worn the black-and-orange – and the Flyers, not the Avalanche, would've won at least the two Stanley Cups Forsberg helped claim in Colorado.

"I remember putting on a Flyers sweater to have my photo taken for a trading card company, but it was only a couple of minutes that I really thought about being with the Flyers," said Forsberg, who was drafted sixth overall by Philadelphia in 1991. "As it turned out, I was just one of a lot of guys involved in that trade. I started my NHL career with Quebec and grew up in Colorado. All I have is great memories there."

Strong, smart, fast and fearless, Forsberg provided boatloads of great memories for those who watched him the most.

"[Forsberg] can do things that guys just can't get done," said Avs teammate Adam Foote in 2002.

Added Paul Kariya, Forsberg's teammate on the 2006–07 Nashville Predators: "He's the ultimate professional, and he makes players around him better. There's no higher a compliment that you can give a player than that. I've never seen him take a shift off."

Forsberg is the sole player in Swedish hockey history to win two Stanley cups, two Olympic gold medals and two world championships, and his career highlights could be split into two categories: what he did on the ice, and what he did to be on the ice.

"My body has been taking a lot of abuse, a lot of beating," said Forsberg in 2001, at a news conference where he announced he would sit out the entire 2001–02 season to rest a body battered by a fearless, power-based playing style and the relentless clutching and grabbing of his opponents.

Back in 1994, when he first joined the Nordiques, Forsberg was happy, healthy and productive. Before he ever played an NHL game, he already had won his first Olympic gold at the 1994 Lillehammer Games, scoring the deciding goal in the shootout – the "stamp" goal against Canadian goalie Corey Hirsch – that gave Sweden the victory. And in the NHL's lockout-shortened 1994–95 campaign, he put up 35 assists and 50 points in 47 games for Quebec.

> "There's Mario [Lemieux] and there's [Wayne] Gretzky that can take time off and do that same thing. I think you put [Peter Forsberg] in that category right now."
>
> – Rob Blake

Forsberg won the Calder Trophy in his rookie NHL campaign – and when the Nords relocated to Denver for his sophomore year, the Ornskoldsvik native relocated his game to equally rare air, scoring 30 goals and 116 points in the only season he played 82 games. He was better still in the 1996 playoffs, netting 10 goals and 21 points in 22 games to help the Avs win the franchise's first Stanley Cup.

Forsberg got his name on the Cup a second time after Colorado won in 2001, but the punishment doled out by opponents had started to take its toll. He played just half of the 1999–2000 season due to shoulder surgery, then had a ruptured spleen removed and was forced out of the 2001 playoffs after the second round.

Thus, when he took the '01–02 season off to heal a myriad of physical woes – including nagging feet problems that would haunt him well into the twilight of his career – it was clear the injuries were cutting into the star center's abilities.

"I've been wearing gel pads and doughnuts around my feet, maybe since 1996," Forsberg said. "So [I've been used to pain] a long time. But [in 2001]… my feet were hurting me every time I got on the ice."

Forsberg returned to Colorado in the 2002 post-season and didn't miss a beat, scoring nine goals and 27 points before the Avs were eliminated by Detroit in the Western Conference final.

Focused on reestablishing himself as one of the game's best, Forsberg lit up the league in 2002–03, winning his first and only Art Ross Trophy – which he locked up by scoring three points in the final game of the regular season – and taking home his first Hart Trophy as NHL MVP.

"It's a heck of a feat," said Avs defenseman Rob Blake at the time. "There's Mario [Lemieux] and there's [Wayne] Gretzky that can take time off and do that same thing. I think you put him in that category right now."

After salary cap constraints forced him out of Colorado in 2005, Forsberg returned to his NHL roots and signed a two-year contract with the Flyers. He had 75 points in his first season in Philadelphia but continued to battle his body and played just 60 games.

When the bottom fell out from under the Flyers in 2006–07 and Forsberg continued to be hampered by injuries, he was traded to Nashville in a multi-player deal. And once the Predators were eliminated in the first round, rumors abounded that Forsberg was considering retirement.

Regardless, his legacy already is clear: Forsberg is a man of the highest skills and standards, a player whose body could be bruised, but never his heart.

"Peter is a big competitor," said former Avs teammate Ville Nieminen. "He always wants to play 100 percent. Nothing else is good enough for him."

– AP

25

Ron Francis

All-star and a Gentleman

Ron Francis provided a portent of things to come on the first day of his first training camp with the Hartford Whalers in 1981. Shortly after taking to the ice, Francis skated up to Whalers veteran Blaine Stoughton and asked if there was anything Stoughton wanted him to do.

"Yeah," was the response, "work both corners."

"OK, I'll try," was the reply.

"I suspected then that he might be a good player," Stoughton recalled later in Francis's rookie season.

Francis helped Stoughton score 52 goals in 1981–82 – the young center amassed 45 assists and 68 points in 59 games as an NHL freshman, in fact – and spent the rest of his career making teams and players better. One of the most effective two-way talents of his era, Francis forged a career based on equal levels of skill, hard work and unselfishness, the last of which came from growing up in a working class family in Sault Ste. Marie, Ont.

"My dad was a steelworker in the plant in the Soo, and he always instilled in me the value of hard work," Francis said. "And it's a well-documented story about my brother and his issues."

Ron's younger brother, Ricky, is intellectually challenged, and growing up with him taught Francis the importance of compassion and understanding. Ricky would later win a gold medal in cross-country skiing at the Special Olympics while wearing one of Ron's Stanley Cup rings.

Francis hit the 30-goal mark only three times during his 23-season career and eclipsed 100 points only three times as well, but was known as one of the most reliable players at either end of the ice. That he won the Selke Trophy only once, in 1995, is something of a mystery. Part of what made Francis so effective was that he could not only score points, but he could also check the opposing team's top center without taking penalties. Francis won the Lady Byng Trophy three times during his career – only Frank Boucher, Red Kelly and Wayne Gretzky have won it more often.

Even though Francis was a model citizen on and off the ice, his career wasn't without controversy. In 1990–91, for example, the Whalers mismanaged Francis so badly that it resulted in the worst trade in franchise history and a deal that is remembered as the biggest steal ever at the trade deadline.

Coming off a 101-point season in 1989–90, Francis was struggling in Hartford, for the first time in his career. Both GM Ed Johnston and coach Rick Ley publicly questioned Francis's leadership ability and motivation and blamed him for the team's ineptitude. Ley decided to strip Francis of the captaincy and called him into his office to deliver the news. He asked Francis to hold off for a day before speaking publicly, but Francis told his teammates because Ley would not. The news leaked out, and it led to Francis, along with Ulf Samuelsson and Grant Jennings, being dealt to the Pittsburgh Penguins for John Cullen, Jeff Parker and Zarley Zalapski.

> "My dad was a steelworker in the plant in the Soo, and he always instilled in me the value of hard work."
>
> – Ron Francis

Even though Francis went on to help the Penguins capture consecutive Stanley cups, the sting of being publicly humiliated and traded away was not an easy one to absorb.

"The first thing you think of is, 'I failed. I wasn't good enough to play my whole career here,' " Francis said.

Many observers point to that deal as the beginning of the end for the Whalers, a move that led to their downward spiral and resulted in the team leaving Hartford for North Carolina, where Francis returned as a free agent and had some very productive years late in his career.

The Penguins, a swashbuckling bunch of offensive talents who had little regard for defense, quickly learned how valuable Francis could be. He stepped into the second line center role and flourished in Pittsburgh.

"When I got to Pittsburgh, [coach] Bob Johnson called me into his office for a chat," Francis said. "He told me, 'You may have heard about this kid we have in our lineup, his name is Lemieux.' And I said, 'Yeah, I know.' And he said, 'Well, he's our No. 1 centerman.' And I said, 'Yeah.' And he said, 'That doesn't mean you can't help us,' and I said, 'I understand exactly where you're going with this, but I'm OK with it.'

"I remember going for a bite to eat with Ulfie a few days after the trade and saying, 'I think this team can win the Cup.' People might forget that Jaromir Jagr was our third line right-winger that year."

Francis forged his career as a Hall of Famer in his eight years with the Penguins, then signed with the Hurricanes and was the public face of the relocated franchise until he was dealt to the Toronto Maple Leafs at the trade deadline in 2003–04. The Canes made the final once with Francis as their captain, but he wasn't able to deliver a Stanley Cup to the Deep South. However, Francis still lives in Raleigh and has been instrumental in working with the Hurricanes to develop a AAA minor hockey program.

All in all, not bad for a player who was one of the select few to wear Cooperalls during his NHL career.

"I guess that didn't really catch on," Francis said.

– KC

Ron Francis Fast Facts

NHL career:	1981–2004
Teams:	Hartford, Pittsburgh, Carolina, Toronto
Post-expansion stats:	549 goals, 1,249 assists, 1,798 points in 1,731 games
Playoff stats:	46 goals, 97 assists, 143 points in 171 games
Individual awards:	
• Selke Trophy	('95)
• Lady Byng Trophy	('95, '98, '02)
• Clancy Memorial Trophy	('02)
First-team all-star berths:	0
Second-team all-star berths:	0
Stanley Cups:	2
Legacy:	A classy leader and playmaker who delivered in the clutch.

26

Scott Stevens

Captain Crunch

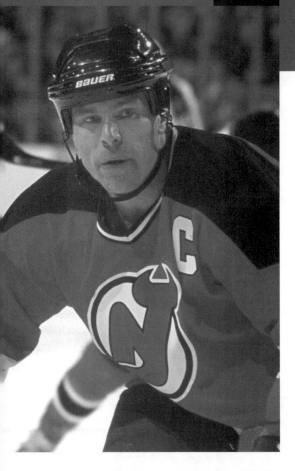

Nobody could've taught Scott Stevens how to knock the sense, and often the consciousness, out of his opponents. But very early in his NHL career, long before he became an integral component and captain of three New Jersey Devils Stanley Cup-winning teams, he learned a lesson that would help him remain one of the game's premier defensive forces for more than two decades.

"I really believe [Stevens is] starting to understand his presence is enough," Capitals coach Bryan Murray told *The Hockey News* in 1984, when Stevens was still a raw rookie. "I don't want to take all the fire out of him. I just don't want him getting carried away and getting in trouble.

"He doesn't have to be intimidating through words or going at it with fists."

Stevens grew up in Kitchener, Ont., and took to hockey at a very young age.

"I've been playing since I was four years old," he said. "All we did was play hockey. We lived by a ski hill in Kitchener, and we never skied… We had an outdoor rink we made and that's all we did."

A star on defense for his hometown Rangers, Stevens was named the OHL's best bodychecker in 1982, the same year the Capitals took him with the fifth overall pick in the NHL entry draft.

> "His presence was unbelievable. Teams feared him."
>
> – Jay Pandolfo

Scott Stevens Fast Facts

NHL career:	1982–2004
Teams:	Washington, St. Louis, New Jersey
Post-expansion stats:	196 goals, 712 assists, 908 points in 1,635 games
Playoff stats:	26 goals, 92 assists, 118 points in 233 games
Individual awards: • **Conn Smythe Trophy**	 ('00)
First-team all-star berths:	2 ('88, '94)
Second-team all-star berths:	3 ('92, '97, '01)
Stanley Cups:	3
Legacy:	Physical blueliner changed careers with his thundering bodychecks.

He made the jump from junior to the NHL right away, amassing nine goals and 25 points in his rookie season of 1982–83. And he established himself as a no-nonsense type of player, accumulating 617 penalty minutes in his first three seasons with Washington.

"I'm serious in games, and I'm serious in practise," said Stevens at the time. "You've got to be serious in practise or you tend to relax, and that's not good."

Added Murray: "Scott doesn't like to be outplayed in any situation."

In nine seasons with the Caps, Stevens developed into a two-way, bone-rattling blueliner. The value of such a player was immense, so when the St. Louis Blues surrendered five first-round draft picks to sign him as a restricted free agent in 1990, many NHL GMs understood.

Fate changed Stevens' career course a little more than a year later. When St. Louis signed Brendan Shanahan, another restricted free agent, away from New Jersey, the two teams were unable to agree on compensation.

The Blues offered Curtis Joseph, Rod Brind'Amour and two draft picks; the Devils wanted Stevens. New Jersey got its way, and although Stevens initially was reluctant to report to the Devils, he was their captain by his second season with the team.

Squarely in his prime when he joined New Jersey, Stevens set a Devils record with 60 assists in 1993–94. And, in 1995, his thunderous hits in the final on Red Wings forwards Slava Kozlov and Keith Primeau were key to New Jersey's first Stanley Cup.

Unlike some players who have won more than one Cup, Stevens said the first win wasn't any sweeter than the other two.

"All of them were very special," he said in 2006, when the Devils retired his No. 4 jersey. "The first one in 1995, I had already been in the league about 14 years, so when it takes that long you start to wonder if it's ever going to happen."

Just as Murray had predicted, Stevens' presence eventually became enough to make a difference. In his final eight seasons, he never had more than 100 penalty minutes, but teammates and opponents alike respected his physical capabilities.

"His presence was unbelievable," said Jay Pandolfo, Stevens' teammate for eight seasons in New Jersey. "Teams feared him. They knew he was on the ice and they had to keep their heads up and be ready for anything.

"Then you had his leadership, the way he played every game the same way… He didn't care whether it was a pre-season game or Game 7 of the Cup final. You knew he was going to give his best, and you knew he expected the same thing from you.

"He didn't have to say anything, he'd just give you a look. He was an ultimate warrior."

Stevens' finest individual achievement came during the Devils' 2000 Cup run, when he laid out several players – most notably, Philadelphia's Eric Lindros in the semifinal – with devastating bodychecks en route to being named playoff MVP.

"It's unbelievable," said Stevens of being awarded the Conn Smythe Trophy. "You dream of winning the Cup and being a big part of it. If you look at the people who've won that trophy in the past, to be included with them, it's something I'll never forget."

After winning his third Cup in 2003, Stevens sustained a concussion that caused him to miss the second half of the 2003–04 campaign. He retired in 2005 and is expected to be a lock for induction into the Hall of Fame.

And that famous presence of his? It remains sorely missed.

"You don't replace Scott Stevens," Pandolfo said. "He was one of a kind."

– AP

27

Gilbert Perreault

The Sublime Sabre

I n the years before Gilbert Perreault was drafted, the Montreal Canadiens had exclusive rights to the top French-Canadian junior players. And the year after Perreault was drafted, the Canadiens robbed the California Seals in a trade that landed them the first pick and future superstar Guy Lafleur.

That one year in between, in 1970, along came Perreault, a great player with a swooping stride, sublime vision and an uncanny ability to stickhandle and create offensive opportunities.

But he had a terrible sense of timing.

Had Perreault been born one year earlier, he would have joined the Canadiens for the first of their six Stanley cups in the 1970s and would have arrived just in time to pick up the torch from the not-so-failing hands of Jean Beliveau, his idol and fellow product of the hockey factory in Victoriaville, Que.

It was in Victoriaville that Perreault, who didn't skate until he was eight, honed the wonderful individual skills that would make him one of the most talented players to ever grace a sheet of ice.

"When I was a kid, we would play games at the rink, and we had enough people for three teams," Perreault said. "I would try to stickhandle through everybody. And when I was in peewee, I was playing peewee, bantam and midget, so on Saturdays I was playing three games at three different levels in one day."

Instead of heading straight to the Canadiens, Perreault was draft-eligible in 1970, the first year of the second wave of expansion and the first in which the NHL did not give the Canadiens the first two picks in the draft. The league also ensured the Canadiens would not get Perreault by passing a rule that prohibited the Buffalo Sabres and their expansion cousins, the Vancouver Canucks, from trading their first-round picks and forcing them to keep the player for at least three seasons.

That set in motion a spectacular individual career for Perreault that is remembered as much for what he wasn't able to accomplish as for what he was able to do. As great as Perreault was for the first decade of his career, he couldn't deliver a Stanley Cup to the Sabres. And due to that perceived shortcoming, he acquired a reputation as a player who couldn't be counted upon when things mattered most.

It didn't help that, along with Vic Hadfield, Jocelyn Guevremont and French Connection linemate Rick Martin, Perreault left the Canadian team in the middle of the 1972 Summit Series against the Soviets after playing only two games. Both he and Martin were under pressure from Buffalo GM Punch Imlach to report to training camp – and did so with Team Canada's blessing, but that didn't stop the public from labeling them as traitors.

In his book *The Game,* Ken Dryden observed that Perreault was not a player who could lead his team to a title.

> **"When I was a kid, we would play games at the rink, and we had enough people for three teams. I would try to stickhandle through everybody."**
>
> **– Gilbert Perreault**

"A best player has followers and must be a leader. He must have the character and personality to match his skills," Dryden wrote about the 1975 Stanley Cup final in which Philadelphia defeated the Sabres in six games. "That's why the Flyers won and the Sabres didn't."

Perreault maintains the Sabres were always "two or three players away" from being a serious Cup threat, but acknowledges that circumstances also conspired against him.

"When I played junior in Montreal, we won two Memorial cups in three years," Perreault said. "We had great teams, and it wasn't just one guy. Most times, it's a matter of being in the right place at the right time. There are many great players who have never won a championship."

Perreault likely could have won the Stanley Cup that eluded him had he taken a different path late in his career. Perreault abruptly retired after the 1985–86 season but was being wooed by the Edmonton Oilers, who had already won two Stanley cups and would go on to win three more. Despite a chance to play on a line with Wayne Gretzky and Jari Kurri, Perreault instead decided to return to the Sabres, but then retired for good after playing just 20 games in 1986–87.

After his last game, he simply said goodbye to his teammates, left the rink and never returned as an active player.

"It was enough for me… I was not very happy with the way I was playing, and I lost very quickly the desire to play," said Perreault at the time. "I am going to play just for fun. No more pressure anymore."

Ah, yes, the pressure. There were many who felt Perreault couldn't handle the pressure of being the go-to player on a championship team. Even Perreault himself acknowledged late in his career that he likely could have accomplished more.

"I think I've had a good career for the 16 years I've played so far," he said in his final full NHL season, "but I think it could have been better."

– KC

Gilbert Perreault Fast Facts

NHL career:	1970–87
Teams:	Buffalo
Post-expansion stats:	512 goals, 814 assists, 1,326 points in 1,191 games
Playoff stats:	33 goals, 70 assists, 103 points in 90 games
Individual awards:	
• Calder Trophy	('71)
• Lady Byng Trophy	('73)
First-team all-star berths:	0
Second-team all-star berths:	2 ('76, '77)
Stanley Cups:	0
Legacy:	The most talented offensive player in Sabres history.

28

Bernie Parent

Bully Backstopper

N HL expansion was very good to a lot of hockey players looking for the chance to prove themselves. It may have been the best to Bernie Parent.

"When you look back, expansion was great for the game, and my timing was just right," said Parent, a Hall of Fame goalie who led the Philadelphia Flyers to back-to-back Stanley cups in 1973–74 and '74–75. "I'll never forget the short time I played in Toronto, and Dave Keon told me one time, 'If you win a Stanley Cup, things will happen to you beyond your wildest dreams.'

"At the time, when somebody shares that with you, you wonder where they're coming from, what they're talking about. But when we won those two years in Philly, I realized how right Dave Keon was."

In the two years he won Cups with Philadelphia, there simply was no better goalie in the league than Parent. The Montreal native won the Conn Smythe and Vezina trophies in both seasons and set a league record for wins in a season (47) that stood for 33 years. (Martin Brodeur, aided by 10 shootout victories, won 48 games in 2006–07.)

Parent's Flyers were the infamous Broad Street Bullies, but nothing was broader than their goalie's shoulders, which the team rode heavily – and never more so than in their first Cup win, when Parent allowed just eight goals in six games and shut out Boston 1-0 in Game 6 to clinch the series.

"A lot of players say it, but I had a lot of help," said Parent, who had a stunning 1.89 goals-against average for the Flyers in '73–74. "I'm very grateful that I played for the best organization in the NHL. Hockey in general was blessed with a guy like [owner] Ed Snider at the helm in Philadelphia. He picked the right people and he was instrumental to our success. He was the catalyst."

Parent acknowledged the Flyers were physical, but noted there was much more to them than simple brute force and intimidation.

"Yeah, we were tough, but we had a lot of skilled players too," he said. "That's the only way you're going to win a championship. What made us special was that we were there for each other and protected ourselves. That made us so tough to play against and was a key reason why we had success on the ice."

Parent didn't see a lot of success early in his NHL career, compiling a 15-32-5 record in the Original Six with Boston in 1965–66 and '66–67. After the Flyers selected him in the 1967 expansion draft, his fortunes would turn for the better – although not right away.

In his first tour with Philadelphia, Parent improved his GAA over three-plus seasons but couldn't do anything about up-and-coming Flyers goaltending prospect Doug Favell. So when GM Keith Allen shipped Parent to the Maple Leafs midway through the 1970–71 campaign – in a three-way deal with Boston that put Rick MacLeish in a Flyers uniform – he was devastated.

> "What made us special was that we were there for each other and protected ourselves."
>
> – Bernie Parent

"I took it very hard," said Parent, who was inducted into the Hall of Fame in 1984, making him the first Flyer ever to receive the honor. "I hated to leave Philly, and it made me think long and hard about where my career was going. But in Toronto, I got to learn from my childhood hero Jacques Plante, and that was one of the best things that ever happened to me."

Plante helped improve Parent's confidence, both on the ice and off it. In fact, Parent took a chance no other NHLer had dared to take when he became the first to sign with the upstart World Hockey Association.

Parent played one year with the WHA's Philadelphia Blazers but quit the team in the playoffs in a contract dispute and, after a showdown with Leafs owner Harold Ballard, engineered a trade back to the Flyers for the start of the '73–74 season.

"I had some hard feelings toward the Flyers when they traded me, but when I went back, I put all of that in the past," Parent said. "I could see we were on the verge of good things, and I was more focused than I'd ever been on winning a Cup. Fortunately for me, the Cups came quickly after I got back."

So did the accolades and adoration.

"The first time we won the Cup, they were expecting 100,000 people to come out and celebrate," said Parent, who was the first pro athlete to grace the cover of *Time* magazine, in 1974. "There wound up being more than two million in the crowd. The city just went wild, and that was a heck of an experience. It was so beautiful."

Parent's career came to an end in 1979, when a stick caught him in the eye and caused permanent damage. He was only 34, but said he was never bitter about leaving the game when he did.

"When I look back at my career, things turned out pretty good," Parent said. "I was able to play 15 years, and that's a long time.

"Would I have played a few more years if I could? Of course. But when I look back, I was fortunate to have played on a team that won two Stanley cups. Some guys are in the league 20-plus years without winning one. So I was lucky."

– AP

Bernie Parent Fast Facts*

NHL career:	1965–79
Teams:	Boston, Philadelphia, Toronto
Post-expansion stats:	271-198-121 record, 2.54 GAA, 54 shutouts in 608 games
Playoff stats:	38-33 record, 2.42 GAA, 6 shutouts in 71 games
Individual awards:	
• Conn Smythe Trophy	('74, '75)
• Vezina Trophy	('74, '75)
First-team all-star berths:	1 ('75)
Second-team all-star berths:	0
Stanley Cups:	2
Legacy:	Only goalie in league history to win back-to-back Conn Smythe trophies.

Fast Facts does not include any pre-expansion statistics or information.

29

Ken
Dryden

Renaissance Man

I t is fair to say Ken Dryden was as good a hockey player as he was a writer. And if you ever watched him play or read his words, you'd know that is the highest praise for the player and poet in him.

Dryden played just seven full NHL seasons, yet influenced hockey to an extent that cannot be overstated. He was brilliant tending goal on six Montreal Canadiens Stanley cup winning teams, just as he was in his ruminations on the game, which culminated in his authorship of the classic hockey book, *The Game*.

Dryden's story began in the Toronto suburb of Etobicoke, Ont., where he grew up with more interests than simply stopping pucks. The rangy, 6 foot 4, future Hall of Famer attended Cornell University and graduated with a history degree. Oh yes, and he also found time to backstop the Big Red to an NCAA championship in 1967, as well as three straight ECAC titles.

Initially drafted 14th overall by the Bruins in 1964, Dryden refused to join the franchise and was traded to Montreal for Guy Allen and Paul Reid. Once he finished university, he began his pro career with the AHL's Montreal Voyageurs in 1970–71.

> **"It is a rare feeling when expectations and hopes, when a team, a game, and I, come together."**
>
> **– Ken Dryden**

His apprenticeship was short, as he was recalled by the Canadiens late in the '70–71 schedule and ended the regular season with a 6-0-0 record and 1.65 goals-against average. But in the playoffs, Dryden was even better.

He was the clear-cut MVP in Montreal's first-round victory over Boston (whose star player, Phil Esposito, called Dryden a "giraffe") and rode his 3.00 GAA to his first Conn Smythe Trophy and Stanley Cup championship.

A typically humble NHLer, Dryden deflected the praise that came his way towards his equally talented teammates.

"Life is easier for the goaltenders with the Canadiens," Dryden told *The Hockey News* at the time. "He does not face as many shots. He has good players in front of him. His side scores a lot of goals. He is usually working on the lead. His side usually wins. It is very nice."

Dryden still had rookie status in 1971–72, and proved his playoff run wasn't a fluke by capturing the Calder Trophy as the league's best freshman. He went 39-8-15 with a 2.24 GAA, and, although the Canadiens lost to the Rangers in the first round, it was clear the kid some likened to an on-ice octopus was a huge part of the Habs' future.

Ken Dryden Fast Facts

NHL career:	1970–79
Teams:	Montreal
Post-expansion stats:	258-57-74 record, 2.23 GAA, 46 shutouts in 397 games
Playoff stats:	80-32 record, 2.40 GAA, 10 shutouts in 112 games
Individual awards:	
• **Conn Smythe Trophy**	('71)
• **Calder Trophy**	('72)
• **Vezina Trophy**	('73, '76, '77, '78, '79)
First-team all-star berths:	5 ('73, '76, '77, '78, '79)
Second-team all-star berths:	1 ('72)
Stanley Cups:	6
Legacy:	Short career filled with championships, individual laurels.

However, after he represented Canada at the 1972 Summit Series and won his first of five Vezina trophies and second Stanley Cup in 1972-73, Dryden stunned the world by announcing his retirement at age 26.

It wasn't injury or skill erosion that prematurely drove Dryden to the sidelines. It was a contract dispute with the team, and it caused him to sit out the entire '73–74 campaign in protest.

He spent the year gaining the requisite experience to attain a degree in law, a goal he had spoken of often for many years. But he railed against the notion he could leave the game behind for another industry, another arena of competition.

"Although I am considered an intellectual, I am really rather physical," Dryden said. "While I am looking forward to leading another kind of life, I am not looking forward to leaving the athletic life."

Within two years of Dryden's return to Montreal, the Canadiens were back hoisting the Cup again, beating Philadelphia in 1976 for their first of four straight championships. And Dryden still was a central part of their winning ways. He tied a team record with 42 wins in '75–76 and went 41-6-8 the following year, when the Habs lost just eight games all season.

At that point, Dryden was growing restless.

"I didn't enjoy the [1976–77] season very much because I have been spoiled by success," he said. "We won too many games too easily. There were times when we'd have to psych ourselves to go into games with spirit… it is simply no fun beating anyone who is easy to beat on any level."

Two years later, he retired for the final time.

"It is a rare feeling when expectations and hopes, when a team, a game, and I, come together," Dryden wrote of the late stage of his career in *The Game*. "After eight years and nearly 500 games, after those hopes and expectations have been battered and mocked, it is rarer still. So each time it happens, each time I get the feeling, I guard it and nourish it, feeling it for as long as I can."

When he published *The Game* in 1983, Dryden gave the hockey community a timeless work of nonfiction. And his contributions to the greater public good did not end there; he also has written about education, as well as amateur hockey, and in 2004, he became a federal Canadian politician.

Dryden's interests always stretched beyond the ice, but his passion for hockey never waned – and neither did the philosophy the game ingrained in him, which he wrote of in describing a Canadiens teammate.

"If you want a team game," Dryden wrote, "where the goal is the team and the goal is to win, you need a player with an emotional and practical stake in a team game, a player to remind you of that game, to bring you back to it whenever you forget it, to be the playing conscience of the team. Like Bob Gainey."

And, like Ken Dryden.

– AP

30

Peter Stastny

Peter the Great

P eter Stastny remembers having a copy of *Time* magazine taken away from him when he was a teenager because it had Slovak reformer Alexander Dubcek on the cover. So when the brown package would arrive at his house, usually from somebody in Montreal, Stastny would treat it as he would a bar of gold.

In it were issues of *The Hockey News*, usually months, sometimes years old. But that didn't stop Stastny and his friends from devouring every name and picture, even if they couldn't read the words.

"We couldn't believe it... a paper that covered only hockey," Stastny said. "And with color pictures of Bobby Hull, Bobby Orr and Stan Mikita, who was my hero. These were sacred papers. We treated them like they were the Bible."

Forty years later, Stastny truly is a man of the world, a Hall of Famer who went on to become Slovakia's representative in the European parliament. A true testament to how the world has changed can be seen in that Stastny played for the former Czechoslovakia in several world championships and the 1976 Canada Cup, played for Canada in the 1984 Canada Cup, and finished his illustrious career representing Slovakia in the 1994 Olympics and 1995 world championship. His NHL-playing sons, Yan and Paul, both have suited up for the United States in international competition. (Paul also played for Slovakia as a teenager.)

At the forefront of it all was Stastny, who came to North America to pursue his NHL dream after officials with the Quebec Nordiques helped him defect from a tournament in Austria in 1980. It was the stuff of a Cold War spy novel at the time, and helped pave the way for players of all nationalities to have a chance to skate in the best league in the world.

But there was a price to be paid. Stastny and his brothers, Marion and Anton, were subjected to enormous amounts of physical and verbal abuse from opponents. Peter remembers there were nights when he had to drive home with his right hand because his left arm would be black and blue with bruises.

"They used to chop and hold and hook, anything to stop you," Stastny said. "Sometimes I wonder what I could have done if I had played now. They used to call me a job stealer, and that didn't bother me, but my eyes used to go red when they called me a commie. I wanted to kill the guy when he said that. I wasn't a commie, I escaped communism because I hated it so much."

Unlike many players, Stastny gave back every bit as good as he got. He was as tough as he was talented and realized very early on that he would have to create space for himself if he wanted to excel in North America. If that meant driving his elbow into somebody's head, that was fine with him. Early in his first NHL season, Mel Bridgman of the Philadelphia Flyers cross-checked him in the face, and Stastny dropped his gloves. Even though Bridgman knocked him to the ice, Stastny flipped Bridgman over and gained the respect of his peers.

> "Not only is he a great skater, but I think he is the most difficult player in the league to stop from a defenseman's point of view. Even more so than Wayne Gretzky."
>
> – Mike O'Connell

"I didn't really have a choice," said Stastny of his willingness to fight back. "I didn't really have anywhere else I could go."

Stastny scored 30 goals or more in eight of his first nine NHL seasons, but his true value came in his ability to play an all-around game. Stastny led the Nordiques in 1982–83 with 47 goals and 124 points, prompting Montreal Canadiens coach Bob Berry to opine that Stastny was the best center in the NHL, including Wayne Gretzky.

And Berry wasn't alone in that opinion. After all, only Gretzky scored more points in the 1980s than Stastny did. In 1982, Stastny led the Nordiques to a seven-game victory over the Boston Bruins in the first round of the playoffs. At one point in the series, a Boston fan held up a sign chiding "The Stastny Sisters," which Peter said fueled his desire to beat the Bruins.

"After the series, I just said, 'Hey, they lost to a bunch of sisters. What does that say about them?' " Stastny recalled.

After that series, Bruins defenseman Mike O'Connell was effusive in his praise for Stastny.

"Not only is he a great skater, but I think he is the most difficult player in the league to stop from a defenseman's point of view," said O'Connell at the time. "Even more so than Wayne Gretzky."

Stastny never lost that competitive nature. He quit as GM of the Slovak national team because of numerous run-ins with the hockey federation. Stastny said it all goes back to his childhood and his eagerness to thumb his nose at the communist regime. He remembers vividly Aug. 21, 1968, the day the Soviet tanks rolled into Czechoslovakia.

"I remember my father was very worried," recalled Stastny, who was 12 at the time. "My brother was at university and [my father] said, 'I hope he's not in the town square.' I said, 'That's exactly where he should be right now.'

"I guess I was a little rebellious."

– KC

Peter Stastny Fast Facts

NHL career:	1980–95
Teams:	Quebec, New Jersey, St. Louis
Post-expansion stats:	450 goals, 789 assists, 1,239 points in 977 games
Playoff stats:	33 goals, 72 assists, 105 points in 93 games
Individual awards: • **Calder Trophy**	('81)
First-team all-star berths:	0
Second-team all-star berths:	0
Stanley Cups:	0
Legacy:	Trailblazing European finished second to Gretzky in points in the 1980s.

31

Al MacInnis

Blue Line Big Shot

Al MacInnis's legend was forged in large part by his fearsome slapshot. Nevertheless, the elite Flames and Blues defenseman didn't receive as much recognition as he should have for other aspects of his game.

"I don't think anyone gave him enough credit for his defense," said Calgary teammate Joe Nieuwendyk. "He was so smart defensively. Maybe he wasn't a smooth skater like Scott Niedermayer, but he certainly was good positionally, and obviously, outstanding offensively.

"And he was a fierce competitor, one of the best all-around players I've played with."

A native of Inverness, NS, MacInnis spent his late teens in Kitchener, Ont., playing for the OHL's Rangers; he was named the league's best defenseman in 1983.

Even then, though, his game had deficiencies, which explains why he was still around when Calgary picked him 15th overall in the 1981 entry draft. And while his first two attempts to make the Flames fell short, MacInnis swiftly addressed the chief knock against him and became a full-time NHLer in 1983–84.

"His defense is one area of his game that was considered a liability," Flames GM Cliff Fletcher told *The Hockey News* at the time. "With his shot and his ability to pass the puck, we thought there would always be a place for him in the league, if only as a specialist. What's made him into the player that he is now is the improvement in his defensive skills."

There was one particular game that dramatically raised MacInnis's profile.

It was Jan. 17, 1984, and the Flames were playing the St. Louis Blues. MacInnis unloaded a slapshot from well outside the blue line that broke the goalie mask of Mike Liut – and, as Liut fell to the ice, the puck squeaked across the goal line.

"That started [the legend]," said Flames assistant coach Bob Murdoch. "His reputation started right there."

Almost instantly, MacInnis became renowned for his bombs over blue lines. And those who saw his slapshot up close attested to its potency.

"There is hard, then there is MacInnis hard," said Liut, who also noted MacInnis "almost killed me" with the mask-busting shot.

Added veteran goalie Don Edwards: "His is the kind of shot a goaltender fears because it's so hard. The thing with Al's shot is he has good control with it too. Usually, it's a foot-and-a-half high or lower. That's the best place to put it because the toughest thing for a goaltender to move is his legs."

MacInnis was hard-pressed to explain why his shot stood out above all others.

> **"I don't think anyone gave him enough credit for his defense."**
>
> **– Joe Nieuwendyk**

"What makes it so hard?" said MacInnis, who won seven hardest-shot competitions at NHL all-star games. "I don't know if I have the answer. It's mostly timing and co-ordination, I guess... the timing is probably the most important part."

In 1986–87, MacInnis put up the first of seven 20-goal seasons. His regular season production dropped off in 1988–89, but in the playoffs he led the Flames to their only Stanley Cup in franchise history.

MacInnis had 24 assists and 31 points in 22 games during Calgary's championship run and was awarded the Conn Smythe Trophy as playoff MVP.

MacInnis set career highs in goals (28, in 1989–90 and '90–91) and points (103 in '90–91) after Calgary's most memorable season. But, as with many players of his stature, the Flames couldn't meet MacInnis's contractual demands, and he was traded to the Blues in 1994 for Phil Housley and draft picks.

His stellar play continued in St. Louis; in 1998–99, at age 36 and after playing in 10 NHL all-star games, MacInnis won the first and only Norris Trophy of his career.

"Thirty-nine- and 40-year-old defensemen aren't supposed to win the Norris Trophy," said MacInnis in 2006. "But, to me, there has always been something about this game and the competition with the best players in the world and being able to compete with and against players who are 20, 22, 25 or 30 that helped me feel younger than I was."

MacInnis also represented Canada in international play on more than one occasion. He was a member of the 1991 Canada Cup championship team and a two-time Olympian who won gold at the 2002 games in Salt Lake City.

"After 1998 in Nagano [Japan], I never thought I'd ever get another chance at playing in the Olympics," MacInnis said. "And then to see my wife and four kids with me [in Salt Lake] taking turns wearing my gold medal around their neck… priceless."

Just three games into the 2003–04 season, MacInnis was forced off the ice due to complications from a 2001 eye injury that had left him with a permanent blind spot. He would never play another NHL game, retiring in 2005 with 1,274 career points – the third-best total for a defender in league history.

When the Blues raised his No. 2 to the rafters and retired it on April 9, 2006, the weight of his achievements finally sunk in for MacInnis.

"I wish I could skate one more shift, take one more slapshot from the blue line, for the best fans of hockey," he said. "But knowing my No. 2 will forever have a home here is more than I could ask.

"I'm forever a St. Louis Blue."

– AP

Al MacInnis Fast Facts

NHL career:	1981–2004
Teams:	Calgary, St. Louis
Post-expansion stats:	340 goals, 934 assists, 1,274 points in 1,416 games
Playoff stats:	39 goals, 121 assists, 160 points in 177 games
Individual awards:	
• **Conn Smythe Trophy**	('89)
• **Norris Trophy**	('99)
First-team all-star berths:	4 ('90, '91, '99, '03)
Second-team all-star berths:	3 ('87, '89, '94)
Stanley Cups:	1
Legacy:	Physical blueliner best known for booming slapshot.

32

Chris Chelios

Perpetual Commotion Machine

Chris Chelios Fast Facts

NHL career:	1984–2007 (active)
Teams:	Montreal, Chicago, Detroit
Post-expansion stats:	182 goals, 754 assists, 936 points in 1,547 games
Playoff stats:	31 goals, 113 assists, 144 points in 246 games
Individual awards: • Norris Trophy	('89, '93, '96)
First-team all-star berths:	5 ('89, '93, '95, '96, '02)
Second-team all-star berths:	2 ('91, '97)
Stanley Cups:	2
Legacy:	Rugged, talented defenseman has played on the edge from his early 20s through his mid-40s.

 obby Parker could never have realized it at the time, but he set the wheels in motion on a Hall of Fame career while frolicking on the beach back in 1979.

At least that's the way Chris Chelios tells it.

After moving from Chicago and spending two of his most formative hockey years playing in beer leagues in San Diego, Chelios was cut from a college club team, losing his spot because a bunch of Canadian kids were promised scholarships. Soon after that, he was out surfing and bumped into Parker, one of those Canadian kids who beat out Chelios for a spot. Parker asked Chelios where he was playing, and when Chelios said his career was over, Parker suggested he call the coach of a Jr. A team in Moose Jaw, a place Chelios couldn't even find on a map.

Initially the coach declined, but then the team went on a losing streak. So he called Chelios, paid his way up to Moose Jaw and turned him into a defenseman.

Almost 30 years later, Chelios still finds himself in the NHL, owner of two Stanley cups, three Norris trophies and a reputation as a player who has combined talent and nastiness as well as any other player in his generation. He has forged a place among the greatest American-born players of all time and provided an extended run of enduring excellence.

When Chelios retires, he will do so as the all-time penalty minutes leader among defensemen who scored 900 or more points in their careers. He will be just one of four players in NHL history – forwards Dale Hunter, Rick Tocchet and Pat Verbeek are the others – who have 900 points and at least 2,800 PIM to their credit.

When he was at his best, Chelios played like a junkyard dog. Craig Ludwig, who was Chelios's defense partner when both were with the Montreal Canadiens early in their careers, could not have put it any better when he said: "Chris Chelios was put on this planet to play hockey."

Chelios isn't certain he agrees wholeheartedly with that assessment, but he can see the sentiment behind it.

"I don't know if I was *born* to play hockey, but for sure I think I was *meant* to play hockey," Chelios said. "Coming from my background and making it to the NHL, I don't think there's any doubt that I was meant to play this game."

Chelios has played in three Original Six cities and has distinguished himself in each one. In Montreal, he established himself as one of the top defensemen in the game and won both a Stanley Cup and a Norris Trophy before being traded to the Chicago Blackhawks for Denis Savard in what turned out to be a ridiculously one-sided trade. It wasn't because Savard was so bad in Montreal, but it was in his hometown of Chicago where Chelios truly made his mark, winning two more Norris trophies and five berths on either the first or second all-star teams. In Detroit, he won a Cup in 2002, the same season he was named to the first all-star team for a fifth time and led the league in plus-minus at plus-40.

What made it all the more remarkable was that Chelios did all of that in Detroit after his 40th birthday.

A player who was as foolish off the ice as he was talented on it early in his career, Chelios has been the epitome of sustained consistency for more than 20 years. During the lockout in 2004–05 – while most veterans were using the forced hiatus to rest their weary bodies – a 43-year-old Chelios went off to

> "Chris Chelios was put on this planet to play hockey."
>
> – Craig Ludwig

play defense for the Motor City Mechanics of the United Hockey League for the final half of the season. Chelios did not have to go through the rigors of major junior hockey and didn't enter the NHL until he was 22 – which saved years on his body – but all that was likely cancelled out by the fact he was often on the ice for 30-plus minutes per game.

His dedication to the game and to off-ice conditioning is legendary. In the summertime, anyone who works out with him is under strict orders to be ready to go at 6 a.m., regardless of what they were up to the night before. Well into his 40s, Chelios still took great pride in being able to outwork far younger players.

"I can't explain it. I really surprise myself sometimes," Chelios said. "I think the biggest thing is that about five years ago I stopped running and took up mountain biking, and as soon as I started doing that, all my pain went away."

Chelios has been known to deliver pain both on and off the ice. During the lockout in 1994–95, he said publicly that commissioner Gary Bettman should look out for the safety of his family. And following the 2004–05 lockout, he led what began as a small group of dissident players and forced an investigation that led to the firing of NHL Players' Association executive director Ted Saskin.

Chelios said he'll continue playing as long as the Red Wings will have him and that he enjoys the game as much now as he did when he broke in with the Canadiens in 1984, after playing his first of four Olympics for Team USA.

"Every summer my trainer [T.R Goodman] tells me he has some kid who's 20 years younger than I am who is going to beat me," Chelios said. "And the kid never wins. He keeps getting closer every year, but close isn't good enough."

– KC

33

Bobby Hull

The Jet that Roared

When he said, "Every time Bobby Hull walks into a room, every player in hockey should kneel," Chicago great Stan Mikita was talking about the business side of the game.

Still, thanks to a career that was beyond fantastic before and after the expansion era began in 1967, Mikita just as easily could've been referring to the on-ice efforts of The Golden Jet.

As part of his Hall of Fame induction speech in 1983 – the same year that Hull became a member – Canadiens' goalie Ken Dryden perfectly summed up how feared the legendary Hawk was by his opponents.

"To watch him coming at you," Dryden said, "was a moment of frozen terror when all logic and all judgment told you to get out of the net and out of the way of his devastating slapshot."

Although his slapshot was thought to reach speeds of 120 miles per hour, Hull was much more than mere puck-blasting bomber. He was strong, swift, tough as nails, with a stick that had more curve than a California coastal highway. And he had a killer partner in Mikita.

By the time expansion rolled around in 1967–68, he already had accomplished a Hall of Fame's worth of feats.

By 1961, and at the tender age of 22, he had won what would be his only Stanley Cup championship. By 1962, he'd become just the third man in league history to score 50 goals in a single season. By 1965, he was a three-time Art Ross Trophy winner as the league's top point-getter. By 1966, he was the only NHLer ever to hit the 50-goal plateau in more than one season.

You can imagine, then, how a player of Hull's talents feasted on an expanded league that some said had watered down its talent base. Which is not to say the Belleville, Ont., native was entirely pleased to be part of a bigger NHL.

"Expansion was good up to a point, but they've crossed the line," the always-outspoken Hull told *The Hockey News* in 1972.

"The talent is spread so thin and so many unrealistic records are being set, I don't think you can feel the same pride at being a big-leaguer or take so much pride in various accomplishments."

Despite his cynicism, Hull, a 10-time NHL first-team all-star, continued to rack up various accomplishments in the post-expansion era. In 1968–69, he scored 58 goals to set a regular season record. That same year, he finished with 107 points, his best-ever NHL total.

Hull also had a memorable season for Chicago in 1970–71, though not for all the right reasons. Sure, he had 45 goals and 97 points, as well as 11 goals and 25 points in 18 playoff games; the problem was, the Hawks blew a Game 7 lead at home against Montreal in the Stanley Cup final, and his second championship slipped through his fingers.

> "If the Hawks paid Hull what he wanted in early '72, the WHA might not have existed."
>
> – Stan Mikita

"It should have been our turn," Hull once said. "It was ours to win, and we lost it. I felt terrible for a long time after the game, until I decided I was not going to ruin my life over one game… You can only hope you get into a game like that again where you can win it all again."

Unfortunately, that was the closest Hull would ever get to another Cup – in large part because of a financial decision that led to his leaving the NHL for the upstart World Hockey Association in 1972. He left with 604 goals, second only to Gordie Howe among the NHL's all-time leading scorers.

Hull signed a landmark 10-year, $2.75-million contract with the Winnipeg Jets and instantly became the WHA's most recognizable player. As Mikita noted, Hull's departure opened the financial floodgates for other players by legitimizing a rival league against which contracts could be leveraged during negotiations with notoriously cheap NHL owners.

"If the Hawks paid Hull what he wanted in early '72," Mikita said, "the WHA might not have existed."

Hull netted 51 goals in his first WHA season, then set a pro hockey record with 77 goals in 1974–75. He attributed much of his success to Swedish linemates Anders Hedberg and Ulf Nilsson.

"In our first workouts at training camp, I sensed that Nilsson and Hedberg had magic," said Hull, who won two WHA championships in Winnipeg and was the league's MVP in 1973 and '75. "They had great speed and could move the puck. And they had imagination. When one of us vacated a spot, the other switched, and the flow of the line continued.

"I didn't have to do all the work myself, and we worked together naturally."

Because of the politics involved, Hull wasn't permitted to play for Team Canada at the 1972 Summit Series. However, he did don the red-and-white at the 1976 Canada Cup and was a key contributor in Canada's win, scoring five goals in eight games.

Hull stayed with the Jets when the WHA and NHL merged in 1979, but was dealt 18 games into the season to Hartford, where Howe was his teammate. He retired at the conclusion of the '79–80 season with 610 NHL goals in 1,063 games.

"I've left a lot of blood, sweat and tears on the ice," Hull once said.

And memories, Bobby. Golden ones.

– AP

Bobby Hull Fast Facts*

NHL career:	1957–72, 1979–80
Teams:	Chicago, Winnipeg, Hartford
Post-expansion stats:	240 goals, 215 assists, 455 points in 389 games
Playoff stats:	22 goals, 32 assists, 54 points in 48 games
Individual awards:	None
First-team all-star berths:	4 ('68, '69, '70, '72)
Second-team all-star berths:	1 ('71)
Stanley Cups:	0
Legacy:	Pre-expansion great continued his prowess before departing for WHA.

*Fast Facts does not include any pre-expansion statistics or information.

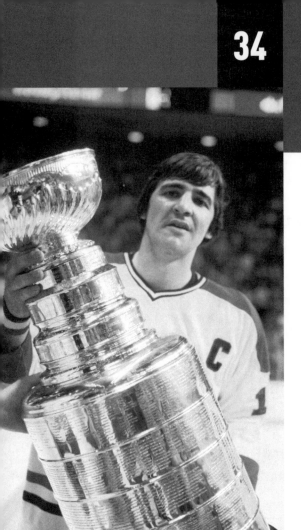

34

Serge Savard

Citizen Canadien

His teammates called Serge Savard The Politician because he had as smooth a set of people skills as any NHLer ever did. But there was no debating the defenseman's grace, grit and superior hockey skills, all of which were on full display during the Montreal native's stunning career with the Canadiens.

"My life in the game has been a privilege," said Savard, whose 17-year career included six Stanley cups (he later won two more as the Habs GM), a key role on Canada's 1972 Summit Series team and a Conn Smythe Trophy in his sophomore NHL season.

"Hockey was our life in Montreal, and I was very, very fortunate to play with the best team, the best organization, one of the best coaches of all time in Scotty Bowman. And I had a lot of respect for the game, my teammates and my opponents over the years. All my life I tried to be a good citizen. I still do."

Part of the Canadiens' famed Big Three on the blue line (along with Larry Robinson and Guy Lapointe), Savard turned pro at age 20 and made his debut in 1966–67 with Montreal's Central League farm team in Houston.

Savard seized an NHL job the following year – in part due to the expansion-triggered departure of many veteran Habs – and never looked back, becoming a hometown legend in 1969 after scoring four goals and 10 points in 14 playoff games and making history as the first defenseman to win the Conn Smythe.

"I was just a happy camper," he said. "I played on a great team that used me in all situations. I won the Conn Smythe Trophy that year probably because I had a lot of points. But anyone could have won it that year. It just happened that I scored a couple of important goals. I don't feel I was the best player of the series, but it just happened that way."

Success came quickly for Savard, but adversity wasn't far behind. In 1970–71, Savard broke his leg in five different places and underwent three operations, missing more than half of the season. He returned the following year, only to break the same leg again.

"I had a bone graft and had to miss a full year after that," Savard said. "I've always been a very confident person and never thought for a moment it would slow down my career. But when I look back today, I think of all the things I did, all the Stanley cups and playing for Team Canada in '72 and '76; I could've missed all that if the injuries I had didn't get better."

> "Hockey was our life in Montreal and I was very, very fortunate to play with the best team, the best organization, one of the best coaches of all time in Scotty Bowman."
>
> – Serge Savard

They did get better, thankfully, and so did Savard. First, he made Team Canada's roster for the fabled 1972 Summit Series; in the five games he played, the Canadians beat Russia four times and tied the other game.

Two years after the injury, Savard put up career bests in goals (20), assists (40), points (60) and plus-minus (plus-71). And, from 1972–79, he was integral to Montreal's five Stanley Cup championships, including four straight from '76–79.

"We were very fortunate," Savard said. "We had players who were skilled, and we were allowed to grow together as a team. The core guys [were] there for a long time."

In 1981, after the Canadiens suffered through a second consecutive early playoff exit, Savard abruptly announced his retirement. Although many believed the years of wear and tear on his body brought about the decision, he denies the choice was all his.

"When I retired in 1981, I was the oldest guy on the team," he said. "They felt like I was the guy who had to go.

"But a player never wants to retire. You always feel you can do the same things you did in the past. You always have that feeling, and it's not true. You could do it one night, but you can't play at that level night after night."

Nevertheless, Savard couldn't resist the lure of playing again, joining former Montreal teammate and then-Winnipeg GM John Ferguson with the Jets midway through the 1981–82 season.

"Fergie kept calling me almost every night that fall until I came back," Savard said. "That was good. They were a young team. I really enjoyed my year-and-a-half there and they really needed veterans. So it was a good fit for both sides."

Savard retired for good in 1983, then made a seamless transition to the management side of the game, masterminding Montreal's Stanley cups in 1986 and '93 as the Canadiens' GM.

"The changeover was easy, because my experience as a player made it easy to be close to the players as GM," said Savard, who received the Bill Masterton Trophy in 1979 for his extraordinary commitment to the game. "Deep down, I was never a manager. I was always a player."

You can say that again.

– AP

Serge Savard Fast Facts*

NHL career:	1966–83
Teams:	Montreal, Winnipeg
Post-expansion stats:	106 goals, 333 assists, 439 points in 1,038 games
Playoff stats:	19 goals, 49 assists, 68 points in 130 games
Individual awards:	
• **Conn Smythe Trophy**	('69)
• **Masterton Trophy**	('79)
First-team all-star berths:	0
Second-team all-star berths:	1 ('79)
Stanley Cups:	8
Legacy:	Two-way blueliner led Canadiens' dynasty on and off the ice.

Fast Facts does not include any pre-expansion statistics or information.

Billy Smith

The Original Money Goalie

It's safe to say there has never been a more feared man to occupy an NHL net than William John Smith. But Battlin' Billy, the same goaltender who once led his team in fighting majors and wielded his stick like a scimitar, didn't have the courage to demand more playing time from his coach.

That's a large reason why you won't find Smith, one of the greatest playoff goalies in NHL history, anywhere near the all-time leaders in regular season appearances, wins or shutouts. While Smith was always the undisputed No. 1 in the playoffs for the dynastic New York Islanders of the early 1980s, he spent almost all of his prime years on the NHL juggernaut sharing regular season goaltending duties, first with Chico Resch, then with Rollie Melanson and Kelly Hrudey.

"That's where I made my biggest mistake, and I think that's where it hurt me big time," Smith said. "I should have made [coach] Al [Arbour] play me more. But you know the old saying, 'If you only knew then what you know now…'"

This was long before the days of Patrick Roy smashing a television and trashing a dressing room for being pulled from a game. Although players were making strides for their individual freedoms in the 1970s and '80s, there was still a long way to go. All of the Islanders players – even superstars such as Bryan Trottier, Mike Bossy and Denis Potvin – were on two-way NHL-AHL contracts, and Smith never saw it as his place to question either Arbour or GM Bill Torrey.

"It was back in the day when the coach was the coach and players didn't undermine him," Smith said. "But I think it was much tougher for me to play every second game than to play every night. And you know who was getting all the tough games…"

Brad Park

Blue Line Cruiser

Brad Park, one of the greatest offense-minded blueliners of all time, considers players of his ilk to be an important but endangered species in today's NHL.

"Blueliners who are good with the puck can make a huge difference in today's game," said Park, inducted into the Hall of Fame in 1988. "Guys like a Scott Niedermayer, like a [Nicklas] Lidstrom are almost always going to make the right play at the right time. [Chris] Chelios is an older version of that type of player. But right now I think the NHL is waiting for the next generation of these guys to come along."

Park first came along in 1965 as a member of the Ontario Hockey Association's Toronto Marlboros. In three seasons, the hometown kid became an immense presence for the Marlies, and he was selected second overall by the New York Rangers in the 1966 amateur draft.

Almost immediately, Park's offensive talents made him a standout member of the Blueshirts. In his rookie 1968–69 season, he averaged nearly a half-point per game; in his sophomore year, he was the youngest Ranger ever to be named to the NHL's first all-star team and was voted runner-up to Bobby Orr for the Norris Trophy.

Park chalks up his successes in Manhattan to teammates who taught him the value of a particular skill.

"When I broke in we had guys who were just tremendous with the puck… Jean Ratelle, Rod Gilbert, Phil Goyette, Donnie Marshall, Bobby Nevin," he said. "What I learned from them in practise was the timing of when exactly a pass should be made. You don't hurry it, you don't wait too long… good timing leads to great execution."

Brad Park Fast Facts

NHL career:	1968–85
Teams:	NY Rangers, Boston, Detroit
Post-expansion stats:	213 goals, 683 assists, 896 points in 1,113 games
Playoff stats:	35 goals, 90 assists, 125 points in 161 games
Individual awards: • **Masterton Trophy**	('84)
First-team all-star berths:	5 ('70, '72, '74, '76, '78)
Second-team all-star berths:	2 ('71, '73)
Stanley Cups:	0
Legacy:	Six-time runner-up for Norris and one of NHL's first offensive defensemen.

Park, whose offensive totals improved in each of his first four seasons with the Blueshirts, also benefited from a legendary coach who believed in his creativity.

"Emile Francis never put the reins on me, never held me back," Park said. "He let me go out there, develop my craft, really grow as a player."

After more than seven seasons in New York – where he became the franchise's all-time leading scorer among defensemen – Park was dealt to Boston along with Joe Zanussi and Jean Ratelle in 1975 for Phil Esposito and Carol Vadnais. It was one of the biggest trades in league history, orchestrated in large part to help the Bruins replace Orr. Park flourished in Boston, putting up at least 50 points in five of the eight seasons he was a Bruin and helping the team reach the Stanley Cup final in 1977 and '78.

"We were close a few times," said Park, also a key member of Team Canada at the famous 1972 Summit Series. "It's not easy to get that far and not win, but you go back and try again every season as long as your body will allow you to."

One of the masters of starting the rush out of his end, Park said his impact came from the imposition of his own will.

> "It's not easy to get [to the Cup final] and not win, but you go back and try again every season as long as your body will allow you to."
>
> – Brad Park

"A lot of times, when guys would try to angle me, I wouldn't allow that," he said. "If I came around the net with the puck and somebody was coming in at me on an angle, I would go straight at him. That way, I was in control more than he was."

By the time Park retired in 1985 at age 37 with the Detroit Red Wings, he had accumulated five first-team all-star honors, two second-team nods, was a six-time Norris Trophy runner-up, and he won the Bill Masterton Trophy in 1984 for his sportsmanship and dedication to the game.

Two decades later, Park's respect for the sport – on full display when he threatened to resign from the Hall of Fame if disgraced former NHLPA boss Alan Eagleson was allowed to remain a member – is still readily apparent.

"As a kid growing up, I was very appreciative of the guys who played in the 1940s, '50s and '60s," Park said. "They were my heroes, and I always had an unbelievable amount of respect for them. And we carried on that sense of history through the late '60s, '70s and early '80s. I knew everybody in the league, and I knew the history of the game. I'm still proud of that."

That said, Park understands the on- and off-ice toll a career in hockey has taken on him. He had his left knee replaced in early 2007, and in 2008, he's scheduled to have the same procedure on his right knee.

That his career would be plagued by knee problems is, he said with a chuckle, something he should have recognized when he was a teenager.

"I was in junior playing with the Marlies, and I had knee problems one year," Park said. "So I went to see the team doctor, Dr. Ball, who was Harold Ballard's brother-in-law.

"Dr. Ball was a gynecologist. That kind of gave me a good indication of the rest of my career right there."

– AP

37

Grant Fuhr

The Fastest Glove in the West

Grant Fuhr's NHL career was not without its rocky moments. But it was his Balboa-esque will to win and outright adoration of the game that made him one of hockey's all-time elite goalies. He also has the distinction of being the first black member of the Hall of Fame.

"I didn't treat playing hockey as a job… Right up until the day I retired, I enjoyed being out there, being part of a team," said Fuhr, who captured five Stanley cups with the Edmonton Oilers from 1984 to '90. "I spent as much time as I could playing, having fun, thinking about the game. For me, that was what it was all about."

After stampeding his way through his junior hockey career – he was 78-21-1 with the WHL's Victoria Cougars – Fuhr was Edmonton's first pick (eighth overall) in the 1981 NHL entry draft. He immediately made the jump to the NHL and, in his rookie 1981–82 season, compiled a 23-game unbeaten streak and finished with a 28-5-14 record.

But then came the first bump in the road: a less-than-memorable sophomore year in which Fuhr injured his shoulder and finished 13-12-5. Still, he helped the upstart Oilers reach the playoffs – and then some.

> "Once you've made it to the NHL, it's pretty likely you're good at stopping pucks. But the way you prepare for the game, the way you see and think the game, I think that's what really sets you apart."
>
> – Grant Fuhr

Edmonton made it all the way to the 1983 Cup final before falling to the Islanders, and Fuhr and his talented young teammates were learning and remembering. And getting better. A whole lot better.

"It's true that you have to learn to lose before you can learn to win," said the Spruce Grove, Alta., native. "Losing is a big part of the process. And by getting trounced in '83, we learned that although we thought we gave a lot, we had to give more."

Fuhr discovered another effective method with which to give, setting an NHL record for goalies by collecting 14 assists in 1983–84.

"I'd like to say I was a playmaker, but a lot of it was kicking rebounds into good places," Fuhr said. "We had a pretty good offensive team, with Wayne [Gretzky] and Mark [Messier] and Paul [Coffey] and Jari [Kurri] and Glenn [Anderson], so I was just a little bit fortunate there."

Grant Fuhr Fast Facts

NHL career:	1981–2000
Teams:	Edmonton, Toronto, Buffalo, Los Angeles, St. Louis, Calgary
Post-expansion stats:	403-295-114 record, 3.37 GAA, 25 shutouts in 868 games
Playoff stats:	92-50 record, 2.92 GAA, 6 shutouts in 150 games
Individual awards:	
• Vezina Trophy	('88)
• Jennings Trophy	('94)
First-team all-star berths:	1 ('88)
Second-team all-star berths:	1 ('82)
Stanley Cups:	5
Legacy:	Acrobatic netminder for Oilers' dynasty in the '80s.

Fuhr's good fortune extended beyond his playmaking potential in '83–84; he also won 30 regular season games and added 10 more in the playoffs to help lead the Oilers to their first Cup. And he won 15 playoff games the following spring to secure Cup number two for Edmonton – and then won 14 games when the Oilers captured their third championship in 1986–87.

Fuhr doesn't agree with the conventional wisdom that asserts that the first time you win a championship is always the sweetest.

"The first one is great, but it's almost more fun to win the second one," he said. "You're so caught up in trying to win that first one, you don't get the chance to enjoy it. The second one, you don't realize how hard it was to win the first one. So each time you win it, you appreciate it more."

After he compiled a 6-1-2 record for Canada during the country's 1987 Canada Cup title, Fuhr had his greatest single NHL season in 1987–88. He played 75 games, won 40, took home the Vezina Trophy and was runner-up to teammate Wayne Gretzky for the Hart Trophy.

What made his skills stand out above the rest? Like many all-time greats, it was his ability to imagine and project his way through games.

"A lot of guys are tied into the technical end of things... I'm more into the mental end of things," he said. "I think a lot of a goalie's success has to do with how you think the game. Once you've made it to the NHL, it's pretty likely you're good at stopping pucks. But the way you prepare for the game, the way you see and think the game, I think that's what really sets you apart."

Fuhr's career hit its most sensationalized pothole when he admitted to substance abuse in 1990 and subsequently was suspended by the league for a year. (He was reinstated after 60 games.) The next season, he was traded to Toronto in a seven-player blockbuster deal. It was the beginning of the second stage of Fuhr's career, one in which he played on four different teams (Toronto, Buffalo, Los Angeles and St. Louis) in five seasons.

Fuhr was 33 by the time he started with the Blues in 1995–96, but his days as a workhorse were far from over. That first season in St. Louis saw him play 79 games, 76 of them consecutively – both remain single-season NHL records.

"I think that year was a good achievement," said Fuhr, who played 73 games the next season. "But honestly, I enjoyed playing that much. You practise every day and players play every day, so why not the goalie? You've got to put the gear on anyways, so you might as well play."

By the time he retired in 2000 – with, of all teams, the Oilers' cross-province rivals in Calgary – Fuhr had a 403-295-114 record and was one of only six goalies to win 400 games in the NHL.

Fuhr can't imagine a better way to underscore a hockey career than by being inducted into the Hall of Fame, as he was in 2003.

"You look at all the accomplishments in my career... the best part is I get mentioned in the company of guys like Glenn Hall, Terry Sawchuk, Jacques Plante," Fuhr said. "It's the company you keep that makes it most special."

– AP

38

Scott Niedermayer

A Champion's Champion

There is an uncanny economy to both Scott Niedermayer's game and his words. In both cases, nothing is done or said superfluously. Expecting him to wax poetic on any subject is tantamount to waiting for him to make a rushed first pass out of the defensive zone.

It's not going to happen.

No player in hockey history is as decorated as Niedermayer. He's the only player ever to have won a Memorial Cup, Stanley Cup, World/Canada Cup, world junior and senior championships and an Olympic gold medal. When asked whether championships follow him around or the opposite is true, Niedermayer had a typical Niedermayer response.

"I'd like to think I helped out a little bit," he said. "Any time you play with a Team Canada, you're going to be surrounded by a lot of great hockey players. And when I was with New Jersey, most of the time I played with Scott Stevens and we had Martin Brodeur, and even in junior we had a great coach in Ken Hitchcock and so many other great players."

Niedermayer is good at many things; giving himself credit is not one of them. Apart from the 1991 world junior championship, which he won as an 18-year-old playing only a couple of shifts per game, he has been an integral part of every title his teams have claimed. It may not seem that way, because what Niedermayer does best just doesn't jump out and scream at people to be noticed, much like the man himself.

Only since he escaped the shackles of the defensive regime in New Jersey has Niedermayer truly blossomed as an offensive weapon. Despite joining the Anaheim Ducks on what was supposed to be the downside of his career, Niedermayer showed no signs of slowing down in his first two seasons in Anaheim.

In fact, the opposite was true. In 2005–06, he had 63 points with the Ducks; in '06–07, he finished with 69. Both were career highs.

Ever since he entered the NHL as a 19-year-old in 1992, Niedermayer has played the game with a remarkable level of consistency. Ducks GM Brian Burke once described Niedermayer's style by saying, "He controls the pace of the game, not our other players and not our opponent."

At his best, Niedermayer has the ability to open up the ice just by carrying the puck for one or two steps. He has the ability to make plays at high speed – although he acknowledged at the end of 2006–07 that some of the quickness was gone from his game – and has the mental resources to think the game at a considerably higher level than most of the players who share the ice with him.

Defensively, Niedermayer has the speed to get back into position before getting into trouble. Opposing forwards often lament that Niedermayer will give them what they think is all kinds of space, and just when the opponent thinks he has a lane, Niedermayer closes the gap instantly and snuffs out any hope.

> **"There were times when I lost some confidence and I would blame myself for things."**
>
> **– Scott Niedermayer**

Prior to joining the Devils in 1992, Niedermayer was a child of the wild hockey that had been played in the 1980s by the Edmonton Oilers and their roving defenseman Paul Coffey. Niedermayer watched and learned from the Oilers and forged a remarkable minor hockey career – he also won at every level as a kid – based on his offensive ability. He continued to dominate that way in the WHL with a powerhouse Kamloops Blazers team and figured that would pretty much continue into his NHL career.

But all that came to a screeching halt with the Devils and their coach, Jacques Lemaire. There were constant meetings between the two, and Lemaire, never a shrinking violet, was direct with Niedermayer and hard on the young blueliner.

"There are always bumps in the road and that was a bump in the road," Niedermayer said. "It was pretty hard for me. There were times when I lost some confidence and I would blame myself for things. Then I would blame somebody else."

If that doesn't sound like Niedermayer, that's because it isn't like him. He learned quickly that in order to succeed in the NHL, he had to improve his defensive game. And while his production with Anaheim suggests his offensive game clearly suffered in New Jersey, his three Stanley Cup rings and long overdue Norris Trophy in 2004 suggest he made the right decision in not bucking the Devils' rigid system. Doing so almost certainly would have resulted in him moving elsewhere early in his career, probably to a place where they don't win Stanley cups.

"At the time, I knew it wasn't what I wanted," Niedermayer said. "I had played a certain style of hockey, and I knew what I was capable of doing. I just had it in my head that I was just going to keep playing that way in the NHL."

It didn't quite work out that way for Niedermayer, the consummate individual talent who morphed into the consummate team player.

"I probably wouldn't have drawn it up this way," he said, "but I certainly can't complain."

– KC

Scott Niedermayer Fast Facts

NHL career:	1991–2007 (active)
Teams:	New Jersey, Anaheim
Post-expansion stats:	140 goals, 468 assists, 608 points in 1,053 games
Playoff stats:	22 goals, 64 assists, 86 points in 183 games
Individual awards:	
• **Norris Trophy**	('04)
• **Conn Smythe Trophy**	('07)
First-team all-star berths:	3 ('04, '06, '07)
Second-team all-star berths:	1 ('98)
Stanley Cups:	4
Legacy:	Wonderful skater, adept passer controls tempo of games.

39

Brian Leetch

The US Defense Core

Here's how this story is supposed to go: Jack Leetch, an all-America hockey player at Boston College in 1963 and one of the last cuts from the 1964 US Olympic team, moves his family from Texas to take a job running the Cheshire Skating Academy in Connecticut. Jack opens up early and stays late every day, prodding and stage-parenting his prodigious son Brian into becoming one the greatest hockey talents the United States has ever produced.

It makes for a good yarn, if only it were accurate. Yes, Jack Leetch did run the local rink in Cheshire, Conn., and was an assistant coach on his son's hockey teams, but to think Brian Leetch grew up a rink rat would be wrong. He honed his talents largely because the teams were so small that they usually only went with four defensemen and the hockey was so raw that Leetch was constantly able to freelance without a system-obsessed, NHL-wannabe coach yammering at him all the time.

In fact, his dad's job at the arena was far more a curse than a blessing.

"The truth is, it wasn't a great job for him or for our family," Leetch said. "He had to do everything there, all the paperwork, run the Zamboni, organize all the ice time. After about seven years of doing it, he basically said, 'This job is hurting my family, and it's killing me,' so he quit and went into sales."

By that time, Brian Leetch was in his teens and was on a career path to NHL stardom. After one brilliant year as an all-American at Boston College, Leetch played in the 1988 Olympics and then joined the New York Rangers, who drafted him ninth overall in 1986, for the end of the season.

Brian Leetch Fast Facts

NHL career:	1988–2006
Teams:	NY Rangers, Toronto, Boston
Post-expansion stats:	247 goals, 781 assists, 1,028 points in 1,205 games
Playoff stats:	28 goals, 69 assists, 97 points in 95 games
Individual awards:	
• Calder Trophy	('89)
• Norris Trophy	('92, '97)
• Conn Smythe Trophy	('94)
First-team all-star berths:	2 ('92, '97)
Second-team all-star berths:	0
Stanley Cups:	1
Legacy:	Greatest US-born defenseman at home in offensive end.

As it always was on the ice, Leetch's timing was impeccable. When he came to the Rangers, his first coach was the fiery Michel Bergeron, who was driven by passion, not systems. It was a perfect fit for Leetch and his style of play.

"There were times when he would look me in the eye and say, 'Brian, we need you. We need you now!'" Leetch recalled. "There were no X's and O's, no, 'Do this, don't do that.' [It was more like], 'Just go out and make something happen.' It was exciting for me, and it was great for me as a young player because I wasn't going out there afraid of making mistakes."

For the next 16 seasons, he starred in New York as one of the smoothest-skating, most efficient defensemen of his generation. He evolved into the face of hockey in the US and became the first American to win the Conn Smythe Trophy as playoff MVP when the Rangers ended a 54-year drought with their Stanley Cup win in 1994.

"I was actually really embarrassed about winning the Conn Smythe," Leetch said. "Everything was a blur on the ice and I heard my name. I went up to Mess [Rangers captain Mark Messier] and said, 'I really feel uncomfortable about this. Can I bring the team up with me?' And he said, 'No way. This is your award. You earned it, now go and get it.' "

> **"I was actually really embarrassed about winning the Conn Smythe."**
>
> **– Brian Leetch**

When Messier arrived in 1991 with the singular mission to deliver a Stanley Cup to the Rangers, Leetch became his roommate on the road. Despite radically divergent personalities off the ice, they meshed wonderfully because they approached the game with the same will to win. Messier, who was the dominant force in the organization from the moment he arrived, was immediately accepted by the Rangers' core group – including the more reserved Leetch, who grew comfortable with the captain very quickly.

"When he first got there, I thought he would be wanting to go out for dinner every night in every city, and I'm not really like that," Leetch said. "One of the first road trips, he asked me where I wanted to go, and I said, 'I'm tired, I'd like to just get room service.' Then on the next trip, he wanted to get room service and that's what we did most of the time. We'd watch games on TV and talk about hockey. I liked going out for beers after games, but he loved it. So that's what we did, and Mark was such a dominating personality, we'd end up hanging out with people we normally wouldn't hang out with."

Leetch's run in New York also was punctuated by stretches of team ineptitude and a long string of non-playoff appearances. His tenure with the Rangers ended in 2004 when he was dealt to the Toronto Maple Leafs at the trade deadline. After some initial bitterness, he embraced playing for the Leafs, even though he saw just 15 regular season games and two playoff rounds before the lockout. He finished his career with the Boston Bruins and, despite offers to return in 2006–07, he left the game in 2006 on his own terms.

"It was very flattering, but it just wasn't in me," Leetch said. "The skating is the skill that usually erodes first, and I could see that happening. Coming back would have been great, but it would only have made sense if I was mentally prepared and if my skating hadn't dropped off. I didn't want to embarrass myself."

– KC

40

Joe Nieuwendyk

Classy Captain,
Classic Scorer

There aren't many men who can lay claim to three Stanley Cup championships and a Conn Smythe Trophy. And there is only one who can boast of three Cups, a playoff MVP award, a Minto Cup national lacrosse championship and Minto Cup MVP honors.

But Joe Nieuwendyk isn't the boastful kind. In fact, he's one of the classiest characters ever to grace the NHL. And he credits his lacrosse glories for helping him succeed throughout his 20-year pro hockey career.

"A lot of my success early in my career involved me standing in front of the net, and a lot of people thought lacrosse helped me with my hand-eye coordination in order to tip pucks into the net," said Nieuwendyk, one of just nine players in NHL history to win a Cup with three different teams. "And I think there's a lot of truth to it… but just being in pressure situations and the physical aspect of lacrosse, those types of things certainly helped me deal with people beating on me when I was trying to score in the NHL."

> "My only problem with the first Cup was I was just 22 years old, so I probably didn't savor the moment like I should've."
>
> – Joe Nieuwendyk

Hailing from Oshawa, Ont., Nieuwendyk grew up idolizing the Toronto Maple Leafs. He spent his formative years in college attending Cornell University, then joined the Calgary Flames, who selected him 27th overall in the 1985 draft, for his first full season in 1987–88.

The 21-year-old center was an instant hit, scoring 51 goals in his rookie season and winning the Calder Trophy as the league's top rookie. But he wasn't prepared for the toll of the relentless NHL schedule – especially as a college player whose Big Red team didn't make the post-season.

"My last year in college, I think we only played 23 games, because we failed to make the playoffs," Nieuwendyk said. "The following year with the Flames, I played over 100 games, when you count exhibition. That was the biggest difference for me."

Nieuwendyk matched his 51-goal output in his sophomore season of 1988–89 – and then ratcheted his game up in the 1989 playoffs, scoring 10 goals and 14 points in 22 games to help the Flames to their first-ever championship.

"My only problem with the first Cup was I was just 22 years old, so I probably didn't savor the moment like I should've," he said. "The thing I took most from it was seeing what it meant to someone like Lanny McDonald, a guy who played 16 years and never got a shot at it before then.

Joe Nieuwendyk Fast Facts

NHL career:	1987–07
Teams:	Calgary, Dallas, New Jersey, Toronto, Florida
Post-expansion stats:	564 goals, 562 assists, 1,126 points in 1,257 games
Playoff stats:	66 goals, 50 assists, 116 points in 158 games
Individual awards:	
• **Calder Trophy**	('88)
• **Conn Smythe Trophy**	('99)
First-team all-star berths:	0
Second-team all-star berths:	0
Stanley Cups:	3
Legacy:	One of two players in NHL history to win Cup with three different teams.

"For him to win it in his last year, it really hit home with all of us. And after that, I didn't get a chance to win another Cup for 10 years."

In between appearances in the Cup final, Nieuwendyk had his share of successes – as well as injuries. He tore an ACL in 1990 at the world championship in Bern, Switzerland, and would deal with bodily breakdowns for the rest of his career.

"I ended up playing eight or nine years without (the ACL)," he said. "I was no different than a lot of guys who've been injured. You just deal with it and move on. My knee was never the same after that injury, but I could still go about what I was doing. You just had to deal with a little discomfort here and there."

Cruelly, after the business side of hockey forced Calgary to trade him in 1995 to Dallas, Nieuwendyk tore his other ACL in the '98 playoffs.

"That was extremely difficult," he said. "I felt good going into the playoffs, felt like I had my game in order, and then to get hurt in the first game was tough to swallow.

"It's funny how things worked out, though. The next year I came back feeling stronger than ever, with two new ACLs, and we won the Cup. Things happen for a reason, I guess."

Nieuwendyk was named playoff MVP in 1999 after scoring 11 goals – including six game-winners – and 21 points in 23 games for Dallas.

"It was an incredible thrill, totally different than the one we experienced in Calgary," said Nieuwendyk of his second Cup. "When I first went there, hockey was not a big deal in Dallas, but we began putting pieces in place, good quality players like [Guy] Carbonneau, [Pat] Verbeek, [Mike] Keane, Eddie Belfour. And to watch the game of hockey grow in a city that was predominantly a football town was quite a thrill for us as players."

After seven years with the Stars, Nieuwendyk was traded in 2002 to New Jersey, where he won his final Cup in '03. His time in New Jersey also saw him claim an Olympic gold medal with Team Canada at the 2002 Games. Following his stint with the Devils, he spent a year in Toronto – "one of the highlights of my career" – and parts of two years with the Florida Panthers before retiring midway through the 2006–07 season.

"I never lost the passion to play, but it was more difficult to get out there on a daily basis, and I didn't want to be a part-time player," he said. "I also had three small kids at home, and for me, it was just the right time to go."

More valuable than his name on any trophy, Nieuwendyk said, was the employment of the team concept to overcome all adversities.

"Winning the Cups was a thrill, but the common denominator of all those teams was you had a group of guys who sacrifice, injure themselves, and lay it on the line for each other," he said. "There's no better feeling than being the last ones standing at the end, and I was fortunate to do it three times."

– AP

41

Bob Gainey

Definitive Defensive Forward

Nobody is exactly certain what Anatoly Tarasov said that day in 1979. We do know this: Bob Gainey was in the midst of his greatest playoff run – one that finished with a Conn Smythe Trophy and the Montreal Canadiens' fourth straight Stanley Cup – and his defensive acumen was at the apex of his Hall of Fame career.

But did the father of Soviet hockey really say Gainey was the best player in the world? Probably not. Over the years, the statement has evolved into Tarasov saying that Gainey was the *most complete* player in the world.

"It has been interpreted a few different ways," Gainey said, "but I sure got a lot of mileage out of it."

It could be argued that Gainey got more mileage out of less natural skill than any Hall of Fame player in history. Sure, he could skate very, very well, and he was strong, and he seemed to think the game on a level higher than most of his peers. His scoring ability was actually underrated during his career – he scored 20 goals four times in 16 seasons and finished his career with a respectable 501 points in 1,160 games – but no elite forward in history defined himself by his ability to defend more than Gainey did.

"There's a lot of dirty work to be done if you're going to win any hockey game," said Gainey during his point-per-game playoff run in 1979, "and I'm one of the guys who goes out and does it. I'm a defensive forward, and if I do my job right, no one scores, so no one notices me."

Gainey did gain plenty of notice by capturing the first four Selke Trophies as the league's best defensive forward, but you get the idea. On a Canadiens team that was full of speed and artistry in the forward ranks, Gainey provided the defensive conscience, and while

161

he was shutting down opponents' star players, the Canadiens' stars never had to face anyone as good as Gainey defensively and were able to display all of their offensive magic.

Gainey said several times during his career that he was glad he never had to face the likes of Guy Lafleur, but he did get a steady diet of players such as Bobby Clarke, Reggie Leach, Darryl Sittler, Lanny McDonald, Mike Bossy and Bryan Trottier. And he shut them down using defensive skills that were every bit as sophisticated as the offensive traits possessed by those whom he was trying to prevent from scoring.

Unlike many checkers who relied on tenaciousness and cheating, Gainey relied on attributes such as superior skating, proper positioning and angling to take quality ice away from his opponents. He combined that with physical strength, with which he was able to keep scorers to the outside, far away from the danger areas.

> **"There's a lot of dirty work to be done if you're going to win any hockey game, and I'm one of the guys who goes out and does it."**
>
> **– Bob Gainey**

Gainey's fate as a defensive force was sealed when he joined the Peterborough Petes, an Ontario Hockey Association junior team coached by Roger Neilson. While Gainey was able to sharpen his defensive skills, other parts of his game suffered.

"In Peterborough, we always had good teams... People would look at our roster and say, 'You don't have many good players, but you win a lot of games,'" Gainey said. "I think where a lot of us missed out, though, was that nobody regarded you as an individual player, and there wasn't a lot of room to explore other areas to develop yourself. As strong as I was in some areas, I was really weak in others. For example, when I went to Montreal, my shooting was a real weakness for me."

Gainey played defense in minor hockey until he was 15, so the foundation on the other side of the puck had been firmly planted by the time he moved to left wing. But unlike many other checkers who reinvented themselves into defensive players, Gainey was born a checker. Guy Carbonneau scored 72 goals in junior hockey and had seasons of 88 and 94 points in the AHL before transforming himself into one of the greatest defensive centers in history. Steve Yzerman went from a dazzling 50-goal scorer to one of the most conscientious defensive players of his era. Sergei Fedorov had seasons of 120 and 107 points when he won his two Selke trophies.

Gainey was nothing like that. His early days were spent playing for the Immaculate Conception Church in Peterborough, and while he was always selected for the church league all-star teams, he was far from the best player. Gainey never felt as though he had to sacrifice offense the way Carbonneau and Yzerman and so many other defensive forwards did, because that skill was never there in the first place.

"I certainly wasn't a latent 50-goal scorer," Gainey said. "It's not like I had to give up anything to play the style that I played."

– KC

Bob Gainey Fast Facts

NHL career:	1973–89
Teams:	Montreal
Post-expansion stats:	239 goals, 262 assists, 501 points in 1,160 games
Playoff stats:	25 goals, 48 assists, 73 points in 182 games
Individual awards:	
• Selke Trophy	('78, '79, '80, '81)
• Conn Smythe Trophy	('79)
First-team all-star berths:	0
Second-team all-star berths:	0
Stanley Cups:	5
Legacy:	The NHL's best-ever shutdown forward did it with class.

42

Cam Neely

Prototype Power Forward

When Cam Neely was a nine-year-old British Columbia lad, he won a minor hockey award for his dedication to the game. Two decades later, the Bill Masterton Trophy he won in 1994 would prove that BC minor hockey committee to be an extremely good judge of character.

"Yeah, it's not the Stanley Cup, but winning the Masterton is a nice way to be acknowledged for how I really felt toward the game," said Neely, Hall of Fame member since 2005 and one of the all-time great Boston Bruins.

In the 13 seasons he spent in the NHL, Neely distinguished himself through two major achievements. Firstly, the Comox, BC, native blossomed into the archetypal power forward, a guy who could bowl you over as easily with his talent as he could with his torso. And, just as admirably, he fought through tortuous injuries to put up numbers that fully healthy NHLers could only dream about.

His rise to the NHL started back in 1982, when Neely was a 17-year-old rookie right-winger for the WHL's Portland Winter Hawks. He stormed onto the scene with 56 goals, 120 points and 130 penalty minutes in 74 games and capped off an incredible freshman season with a Memorial Cup championship.

"Even in my junior hockey days, I knew good things came from playing a physical style," said Neely, who was selected ninth overall by Vancouver in the 1983 NHL entry draft. "For me, the physical side of the game came first, and the offense came from being physical."

At 19, he jumped to the NHL, and his first three seasons with the Canucks were productive, if unspectacular. And for a player who craved to contribute, being middle-of-the-road wasn't good enough for Neely.

It wasn't good enough for Vancouver's management, either, and in the summer of 1986 they dealt Neely and a first-round pick to the Bruins for Barry Pederson. Leaving his home province wasn't tough, however, because he wanted an opportunity to play a bigger role than he had with the Canucks.

"The trade was kind of bittersweet because I wasn't really playing all that much my third year in Vancouver," Neely said. "I was looking forward to coming back the next year and having a better year. But on the flip side, I looked at it like the Bruins wanted me and as a great opportunity to see what I could do [in Boston], as opposed to trying to convince people in Vancouver that I was more than what they thought."

Neely was an instant hit in Beantown – as a dangerous sniper who could also hit and fight – posting personal bests in goals (36), assists (36), points (72) and penalty minutes (143) in his first season with the Bruins. And the next season, he set a new benchmark for goals (42) while leading Boston to its first appearance in the Stanley Cup final in 10 years.

> "For me, the physical side of the game came first, and the offense came from being physical."
>
> – Cam Neely

The Wayne Gretzky-led Edmonton Oilers swept Neely's Bruins in the final. And although his team clearly was overwhelmed by the fearsome force of Edmonton's attack, Neely's disappointment was not muted whatsoever.

"It's easier to lose in the first round than it is in the final," he said. "You get that far, you battle that long with your teammates, you get that close to winning the ultimate prize… it's very, very disappointing when you don't."

Neely had his best pro season in 1989–90, potting a career best in goals (55) and points (92), and powering the Bruins to the Cup final for the second time in three seasons. They fell to the Oilers again, this time in five games.

In the 1991 playoffs – after he'd hit the 50-goal plateau for the second straight season – Neely was the victim of a vicious cheap shot from Ulf Samuelsson that changed the course of his career. His thigh, which had been devastated by Samuelsson's leg-on-leg hit, would never be the same – and it ultimately would end his career at age 31.

"It was very difficult to be in a situation where I had to let my body heal," he said. "After that, I was going on pure love for the game, trying to compete at a level I was accustomed to. Not practising much, playing every other game. My knee was not really co-operating, and the pain that went along with that was difficult.

"But what was happening on the ice was so magical, everything I was going through to get to that point was worth it."

What was happening was a 1993–94 campaign in which Neely could do no wrong. Playing more or less on one leg, he scored 50 goals in just 49 games.

"I can't really explain that year at all," Neely said. "Everything I threw at the net found its way in. I remember, even if I hadn't played or practised in a few days, scoring on my first or second shift and coming back to the bench just shaking my head. It was unbelievable."

When he retired in 1996, Neely had 395 goals and 694 points in 726 games. He had his No. 8 retired by the Bruins in 2004 and was inducted into the Hall of Fame the next year. But the best reward comes when he hears his name mentioned by amateurs and pros alike.

"When you hear young kids talking about players they'd like to be and your name is mentioned, it's a great feeling," he said. "And when you hear GMs or coaches say they're looking for a Cam Neely-type player, people have an understanding of what that means. So I'm obviously proud of that."

– AP

Cam Neely Fast Facts

NHL career:	1983–96
Teams:	Vancouver, Boston
Post-expansion stats:	395 goals, 299 assists, 694 points in 726 games
Playoff stats:	57 goals, 32 assists, 89 points in 93 games
Individual awards: • **Masterton Trophy**	('94)
First-team all-star berths:	0
Second-team all-star berths:	4 ('88, '90, '91, '94)
Stanley Cups:	0
Legacy:	Prototypical power forward led Bruins to two Cup finals.

43

Frank Mahovlich

Hesitant Hero

For Francis William Mahovlich, the advent of expansion in the NHL brought on some very, very dark times. But it wouldn't be long before Mahovlich would be freed from his personal prison that was the Toronto Maple Leafs and released into the light.

The 1967–68 season was Mahovlich's last with the Maple Leafs and their dictatorial coach-GM Punch Imlach. Although a brilliant player for much of his time with the Leafs and the one true superstar the organization had, it seemed he never could do enough to please Imlach or the fans.

Mahovlich was one of the most physically gifted players of his era. At 6 feet and 205 pounds, he was considered a behemoth. He had soft hands and outstanding scoring instincts but often struggled mightily to live up to the expectations that had been created.

"Hockey is mostly a streetcar named desire," Imlach once said of Mahovlich. "Sometimes Frank doesn't catch it."

Mahovlich's troubles came to an apex in November of the '67–68 season. With the Leafs ready to embark on a train trip to Detroit, Mahovlich got up from his seat and left the train. Not long after, he was hospitalized for depression for the second time in his career and, according to some reports, had suffered a nervous breakdown.

But better times were ahead for Mahovlich, and they came in March when he was dealt to the moribund Detroit Red Wings. On his way out of Toronto, Mahovlich said, "As to whether I'll be happier in Detroit, I'll have to wait and see. Maybe I'm just not a happy guy."

In his two seasons with the Red Wings, Mahovlich was brilliant and happy, even if the Red Wings were terrible. Mahovlich scored 49 goals in 1968–69 and helped Gordie Howe to a 100-point season. For the first time in a decade, the game was a source of enjoyment rather than a burden for Mahovlich.

"It was the best thing for me," said Mahovlich, now a Canadian senator. "I went to Detroit and had some great success there. But the whole time I was there, we had one NHL-caliber defenseman, and that was Gary Bergman. Aside from that, it was a revolving door, and there really wasn't any direction."

But Mahovlich was personally so happy in Detroit that a trade to the Montreal Canadiens in 1971 upset him to the point where he considered not reporting. Prior to getting on a flight to join the team in Minnesota, Mahovlich spoke with Canadiens' GM Sam Pollock, who told him they would speak once the team returned to Montreal.

> "And as soon as I got with [Montreal], they took to me right away. I scored a goal in my first game, and I could just feel myself gaining momentum right away."
>
> – Frank Mahovlich

"I get off the plane and [coach] Al MacNeil and [assistant GM] Ron Caron are there at the airport waiting for me," Mahovlich said. "I thought, 'This has never happened before. Maybe this will be even better than Detroit.' And as soon as I got with the team, they took to me right away. I scored a goal in my first game, and I could just feel myself gaining momentum right away. It was just an amazing feeling. I felt like nobody was going to be able to stop me."

Even though he was back in the spotlight in Montreal, Mahovlich was far more comfortable in his surroundings and started his career with the Canadiens playing on a line with Yvan Cournoyer and Guy Lafleur. It also allowed Mahovlich to be reunited with his younger brother Peter, who had been discarded by the Wings in 1969 but blossomed into a 35-goal scorer and a terrifically versatile player with the Canadiens.

"What a lot of people don't realize was that Peter was a really skilled player," Mahovlich said. "You should have seen the moves on that kid. One time a reporter asked Sam Pollock what the difference between Frank and Pete was, and he said, 'Frank goes through people, and Pete goes around them.' "

Mahovlich became the first player to score 40-plus goals with three different teams when he notched 43 with the Canadiens in 1971–72, the year after he helped the team win the Stanley Cup. That spring, Montreal finished third in the East Division and knocked off the powerhouse Boston Bruins in the first round, then faced the star-studded Chicago Blackhawks in the Stanley Cup final.

With the Hawks leading the series 3-2 and going into the third period of Game 6 with a 3-2 edge, Frank and Pete scored third-period goals to give the Canadiens the win before Montreal won Game 7 by a 3-2 count in Chicago.

"Jim Pappin [of the Blachawks] still has nightmares about that game to this day," Mahovlich said.

Mahovlich led the playoffs in both goals (14) and points (27) that year and then won the sixth Stanley Cup of his career in 1973 when he scored 23 points in the playoffs. After an 80-point season with the Canadiens in 1973–74, he returned to Toronto, this time with the Toros of the World Hockey Association. He scored three goals in his first WHA game and played four more years before failing in a comeback bid with the Red Wings in 1979.

Mahovlich would have undoubtedly won multiple Cups had he stayed with the Canadiens, but doesn't regret his decision to bolt the NHL.

"The WHA was the only place where I made any real money," Mahovlich said. "Before that, I was making nothing."

– KC

Frank Mahovlich Fast Facts*

NHL career:	1957–74
Teams:	Toronto, Detroit, Montreal
Post-expansion stats:	246 goals, 196 assists, 442 points in 511 games
Playoff stats:	27 goals, 31 assists, 58 points in 53 games
Individual awards:	None
First-team all-star berths:	1 ('73)
Second-team all-star berths:	2 ('69, '70)
Stanley Cups:	2
Legacy:	Rare blend of size and talent hit his hockey peak as a Hab.

*Fast Facts does not include any pre-expansion statistics or information.

44

Pavel Bure

Russian Rocket

It comes as no surprise that Pavel Bure idolized tennis superstar Boris Becker when he was growing up. Both he and Becker shared a dynamic talent for their respective sports, and, like Becker, Bure was forced to leave his game far too quickly.

During the 1990s, there wasn't a player on the planet who possessed Bure's combination of explosiveness and charisma. Listed at 5 foot 10 and 192 pounds, Bure was the first player in more than 20 years to be nicknamed Rocket – he was heralded as the Russian Rocket – and, like Rocket Richard, he captured people's imagination with his flair and goal-scoring prowess.

"When I played, I always tried to create something to excite the fans," Bure said. "When I was a kid watching sports, I was always looking for the guy who would do something different than the other guys would do. I remember watching Boris Becker in his first Wimbledon, and here's this guy diving all over the place for the ball. Everybody remembers those years when he played."

And everyone who was watching hockey in the 1990s remembers Bure's virtuoso performances.

"I'm just like a fan of Pavel's," Bure's brother and fellow NHLer Valeri once said. "I sit there with people at Vancouver Coliseum, and I shake my head. How did he do that? It's crazy, some of the things he does."

Bure's rushes up the ice were legendary, as was his ability to blow by defenders en route to the net. Despite his size, his solid core and low center of gravity made Bure almost impossible to knock off the puck – and there was nobody faster. He remains the only true superstar the Canucks have ever had and reminded many of Gilbert Perreault, the player the Canucks lost a chance to select when the Buffalo Sabres won the No. 1 overall pick with the spin of a roulette wheel before the 1970 entry draft. (Both cities had entered the league as expansion teams.)

There was no player more feared – from a speed and skill perspective – than Bure in his prime. He exploited any gap in the ice, and giving him any time and space was an invitation to be scored upon. Bure also was able to control the puck at warp speed, and when he wasn't blowing by people with his speed, he was stickhandling past them with his skill.

However, Bure played only 12 years in the NHL, with knee injuries finally taking their toll and forcing him into retirement after a brief stint with the New York Rangers in 2003. One can't help but wonder what Bure would have accomplished had he been able to play longer, but Bure doesn't spend his time worrying about such things.

> "When I played, I always tried to create something to excite the fans."
>
> – Pavel Bure

"I don't look at it that way… I think I achieved a lot," Bure said. "I had five 50-goal seasons, and I'm really satisfied with that. Of course you could always do more, like win a Stanley Cup. I never did that."

Bure was unable to achieve that feat, unlike Sergei Fedorov and Alexander Mogilny, his linemates on the Soviet national junior team. (The threesome was unstoppable at the 1989 world junior championship, combining for 19 goals and 38 points in seven games en route to the gold medal).

The absence of an NHL title, however, was not for a lack of trying. In large part due to Bure, the Canucks made it to Game 7 of the Stanley Cup final in 1994 against the Rangers after falling 3-1 in the series. Bure followed up his second 60-goal season that year with 16 goals and 31 points in the playoffs.

Bure was named to a first all-star team just once in his career, mainly because he was always up against the likes of Brett Hull, Teemu Selanne and Jaromir Jagr, three other right-wingers who also were in their primes and establishing themselves as superstars. Still, Bure managed to win the Rocket Richard Trophy as the league's top goal-scorer twice in his career. And after starting his rookie season in 1991–92 late because of a court battle over whether the Canucks had the right to draft and sign him, Bure scored 34 goals and 60 points in 65 games and won the Calder Trophy.

Now all that waits is the Hall of Fame. Bure was eligible for induction in 2006, but was passed over in the players' category in favor of Patrick Roy and Dick Duff. Even though it will be more difficult for him to be inducted in future years because of a logjam for induction, there's little doubt that Bure deserves to be there.

"It would be a huge honor, but it's not something I think about," Bure said. "Other very respected people would have to make that decision. I know what I've done in my career."

– KC

Pavel Bure Fast Facts

NHL career:	1991–2003
Teams:	Vancouver, Florida, NY Rangers
Post-expansion stats:	437 goals, 342 assists, 779 points in 702 games
Playoff stats:	35 goals, 35 assists, 70 points in 64 games
Individual awards:	
• Calder Trophy	('92)
• Rocket Richard Trophy	('01, '02)
First-team all-star berths:	1 ('94)
Second-team all-star berths:	2 ('00, '01)
Stanley Cups:	0
Legacy:	Explosive skater, dazzling stickhandler, dynamic scorer.

45

Tony Esposito

Mr. Zero

In his first full NHL season, Tony Esposito not only won the Calder Trophy as rookie of the year but the Vezina Trophy as the league's top goaltender as well.

Short of adding a Stanley Cup to the mix, does it get any better than that for a rook, Tony?

"I won't lie to you… it felt great," said Esposito, a Hall of Famer and legendary member of the Chicago Blackhawks who also was a three-time Vezina winner and a pioneer of the butterfly style. "You work hard to get to a position where you can succeed, and though I didn't win a Cup when I played, I did have a fair degree of success along the way."

The younger brother of the equally unforgettable Phil Esposito, Tony O played 15 NHL seasons, a feat all the more remarkable when you consider he didn't break into the league until he was 26. By then, he already had graduated from Michigan Tech and played in Houston of the Central League, as well as a short stint in Montreal before the Canadiens lost him to Chicago in the 1969 intra-league draft.

The lengthy apprenticeship gave Esposito the opportunity to develop the butterfly style, at a point in league history when powerful voices in the hockey world weren't believers.

"The press, mainly in Toronto, said you couldn't play that style," Esposito said. "I never focused on being someone who was trying to revolutionize the position. That was just the style that worked best for me.

"And really, it was a combination of little things I'd pick up from other goalies. I always liked Glenn Hall, who was also a reflex-type goalie. I liked Terry Sawchuk's competitive nature, his edge when he was out there. I liked Johnny Bower's poke check. All those things, I tried to include in the way I played."

Esposito also was among the first wave of NHLers whose commitment to physical fitness lasted longer than the season did.

"I always worked out on my own," he said. "I had my own weights, I played racquetball in the summer to keep my legs and reflexes sharp. I was physically fit until my very last game. I could've played until I was 45, and conditioning had a lot to do with how long I lasted in the league."

Once in the Windy City, Esposito immediately excelled – and so did the Hawks, who qualified for a playoff berth in 1969–70 after failing to make it the previous season. Esposito went 38-17-8 in that Calder- and Vezina-winning campaign, with a sparkling 2.17 goals-against average and an astonishing 15 shutouts, a modern day record that still stands. (George Hainsworth recorded 22 shutouts in 1928–29.)

> **"I could've played until I was 45, and conditioning had a lot to do with how long I lasted in the league."**
>
> **– Tony Esposito**

The potential for a turnaround in Chicago – as well as an opportunity to prove his own worth – was noted by Esposito while he was still a member of the Canadiens' organization.

"We beat the Hawks in Montreal, and I won that game," Esposito recalled. "But we were outplayed by Chicago. And fortunately for us, we got two or three bad goals on them. And I was at the other end of the ice.

"But you could see their offensive talent was there. I mean, [Stan] Mikita and Bobby Hull, come on! Their defense wasn't bad either, but their goaltending was below average, I thought. So I got an opportunity, and I thought, 'This is my chance to move in.' And once you're in the door, I learned, you don't let anybody else in."

Esposito had eight seasons of at least 30 wins with the Blackhawks, who never missed the playoffs when he was on the roster. And early in his career, he was rewarded for his stellar play with a coveted spot on Team Canada's famed 1972 Summit Series team.

He went 2-1-1 in the series, and discovered his deep-in-the-net style was effective against the Russians.

"We had no idea about them," Esposito said. "Their style was so different. They didn't shoot until five feet from the net, so there was no need to go out and challenge them."

The beginning of the end came for Esposito when the Hawks brought in youngster Murray Bannerman to split time with the veteran in 1982–83. Esposito, who thrived on a heavy workload, did not find platooning to be an ideal experience.

"I wasn't a part-time guy," said Esposito, who retired in 1984. "I was in top shape, but I couldn't adjust to that, and I just couldn't get that mental edge that way."

Although Esposito never won a Cup, his extended tenure as an elite goalie is a legacy he embraces.

"I was a top goaltender, and I played a long time at a high level," he said. "Ability is one thing, and it's normal to see guys come in and play well for a couple years, then fizzle out. Having longevity, that's a pretty good achievement. And I'm proud of that."

– AP

Tony Esposito Fast Facts

NHL career:	1968–84
Teams:	Montreal, Chicago
Post-expansion stats:	423-306-151 record, 2.92 GAA, 76 shutouts in 886 games
Playoff stats:	45-53 record, 3.07 GAA, 6 shutouts in 99 games
Individual awards:	
• Calder Trophy	('70)
• Vezina Trophy	('70, '72, '74)
First-team all-star berths:	3 ('70, '72, '80)
Second-team all-star berths:	2 ('73, '74)
Stanley Cups:	0
Legacy:	Revolutionized butterfly goaltending style.

46

Chris Pronger

Mr. Big

C hris Pronger cannot pinpoint the precise moment of his epiphany. He knows only that it came with a healthy dose of self-realization and an even healthier dose of Mike Keenan.

Perhaps it was during his first workout with the St. Louis Blues, when his lung capacity was roughly that of a beer league player and Keenan was screaming into his ear. Perhaps it was during one of the almost daily meetings with Keenan, in which Pronger was browbeaten and berated for his off-ice habits. Perhaps it was just prior to the playoffs in 1996, when Keenan told him that he already had a deal worked out to trade Pronger to the Ottawa Senators for Alexei Yashin, "if I didn't get my head out of my ass."

In any event, Pronger finally got it. He took the circuitous route to NHL stardom, but once he found his way, he developed into one of the game's all-time great defensemen. Pronger wouldn't have been the first bright young light to burn out fast and fade away because of unwise life choices, but when he came to the crossroads of his career in that 1995–96 season, he made the right decision.

> **"When you're as competitive as I am and you don't like losing, well... That's when I started really working hard off the ice and I turned things around."**
>
> **– Chris Pronger**

"I had just come from Hartford, which was a nightmare, and here I was in St. Louis... I'm 21 years old and Mike Keenan is beating me into the ground," said Pronger, who was drafted second overall by the Whalers in 1993. "I was lost. All I could say to myself was, 'This is the NHL? I'm supposed to be having a great time, and I'm miserable.'"

That was precisely when his competitive instincts – which have since made Pronger a perennial Norris Trophy candidate – kicked in. Until that point in his hockey career, Pronger could always rely on prodigious skill, enormous size and a nasty disposition to carry him through. But when he got to St. Louis, he had to work at it just like everybody else.

"I said to myself, 'I'm either going to just say screw this, or I'm going to do something about it,' " Pronger said. "When you're as competitive as I am and you don't like losing, well, I felt just like I was losing. That's when I started really working hard off the ice and I turned things around."

He had a few things to turn around in his life. Early in his career with the Hartford Whalers, Pronger ended up in a Buffalo jail, along with a couple of teammates and assistant coach Kevin McCarthy, after a barroom brawl. That same season he was involved in a single-vehicle crash in Hartford and, as well, was convicted of drunk driving in Ohio.

Then there was the NHL lockout – the first one, in 1994-95, that is – and even though Pronger entered the fall of '94 with the best intentions, things fell apart fairly quickly. With no promise of an NHL season in sight and no college experience, Pronger made an admittedly rash decision.

"I figured I would go to university," Pronger said. "I went to Winnipeg, and all my buddies were there. I basically boozed it up for four months and rarely worked out."

So exactly what courses did he take at the University of Manitoba anyway?

"I didn't *go* to university, I was *at* university," Pronger said. "There's a big distinction."

Then came the trade to St. Louis – in exchange for Brendan Shanahan in the summer of '95 – and Pronger's long and painful path to redemption began. He has developed into one of the most dominant defensemen in the league, one who conserves energy better than any other – except maybe his Anaheim Ducks teammate Scott Niedermayer – and can eat minutes the way he used to go through beer pitchers. He has played as much as 42 minutes in a 60-minute regular season game and averages close to 30 minutes per night.

Pronger is a premier shutdown defenseman because of his size, reach and hockey sense, and also possesses a terrific offensive streak that is enhanced by one of the most accurate low slapshots in the league. His two-way dominance hit a high point in 1999–2000, when he captured the Norris and Hart trophies and led the NHL with a plus-52 rating. And whenever Pronger mans the point, his forwards know the puck won't be coming in around their ears; he has the ability to pick the low corners from 60 feet with shots that don't look particularly dangerous.

"I've always been able to do that... Even when the puck is rolling, I can keep it down," said Pronger, a three-time Canadian Olympian who won gold at Salt Lake City in 2002. "One of the reasons that Al [MacInnis] never took one-timers from the blue line was that he could never control it. That has never been a problem for me."

Although Pronger has tamed down his wild ways, controversy is never too far away. He's outspoken and colorful, which sometimes gets him into trouble. During the 2004–05 lockout, he was accused of usurping the union's efforts by going straight to NHL management, and he will be forever vilified in Edmonton for leading the Oilers to the 2006 Stanley Cup final, then turning his back on the city by forcing a trade.

Pronger has never disclosed exactly why he demanded the trade, but he moved on, and things worked out very well for him with the Ducks. He was an integral part of the team's first Stanley Cup championship in the spring of 2007.

"I'm really happy here," said Pronger after his first season in Anaheim. "I feel I'm still growing as a player."

– KC

Chris Pronger Fast Facts

NHL career:	1993–2007 (active)
Teams:	Hartford, St. Louis, Edmonton, Anaheim
Post-expansion stats:	119 goals, 396 assists, 515 points in 868 games
Playoff stats:	18 goals, 69 assists, 87 points in 128 games
Individual awards: • **Norris Trophy** • **Hart Trophy**	 ('00) ('00)
First-team all-star berths:	1 ('00)
Second-team all-star berths:	3 ('98, '04, '07)
Stanley Cups:	1
Legacy:	Five-tool blueliner a big factor in every area of the ice.

47

Dale Hawerchuk

Just Ducky

When Winnipeg Jets GM John Ferguson signed Dale Hawerchuk to his first contract at the corner of Portage and Main in downtown Winnipeg in the summer of 1981, he proudly proclaimed, "We don't intend to be drafting first overall anymore."

Ferguson was proved right. The Winnipeg Jets/Phoenix Coyotes have not chosen first overall since then. Of course, they've never made it past the second round of the playoffs, and the Jets left town in 1996. But none of that can be attributed to a player who was a victim of bad timing and bad teams more than anything else.

As an individual athlete, Hawerchuk was brilliant. Equally artistic as he was effective, Hawerchuk had the ability to make his team better. With the Jets, though, it just wasn't enough to break through the stranglehold on excellence that was owned by the Edmonton Oilers.

By the time Hawerchuk arrived in Winnipeg, he already had been named Canadian major junior's player of the year and MVP of the Memorial Cup tournament. There were very real comparisons being made to Wayne Gretzky – from credible sources.

Serge Savard was at the end of his career with the Jets when Hawerchuk was starting, and, early in Hawerchuk's rookie season, Savard predicted, "He's going to be as good as Gretzky is. Remember who said it first."

Hawerchuk didn't disappoint. He scored 103 points and was named rookie of the year in 1981–82, holding the record as the youngest player to eclipse 100 points until Sidney Crosby usurped him in 2005–06. In his first seven seasons with the Jets, Hawerchuk scored 100-plus points six times and earned his only second-team all-star berth in 1984–85, behind Gretzky.

But while Gretzky had Jari Kurri as a running mate for most of his career in Edmonton, Hawerchuk had Paul MacLean, a Canadian university player and cast-off from the St. Louis Blues who parlayed his partnership with Hawerchuk into six 30-plus goal seasons.

"Playing with Ducky is simple," said MacLean at the time. "You give him the puck at center ice, then head for the right post. Sooner or later, it seems to get there."

But Hawerchuk could never escape the large shadow cast by Gretzky, and later Mario Lemieux. When Hawerchuk signed an eight-year contract extension in 1985, Jets defenseman Randy Carlyle said, "He's demonstrated to all of us that he's the second-best player in the league."

> **"You give [Hawerchuk] the puck at center ice, then head for the right post. Sooner or later, it seems to get there."**
>
> **– Paul MacLean**

From then on, it seemed both Hawerchuk and the Jets were destined for second-class status. But the way Hawerchuk sees it, being No. 2 to the likes of Gretzky is far more of an honor than an albatross.

"I can honestly say that I never once thought about it," Hawerchuk said. "The way I see it, I was lucky to play against him and with him [in the Canada Cup tournaments]. Whenever anyone talks about how great Wayne Gretzky was, I can tell them that I know exactly how great he was. And he opened up a lot of things for guys who were 18. Until he came along, teams really weren't crazy about using 18-year-old guys. But I would look at him and say, 'If he can do it, why can't I?' "

The Jets won just one playoff series with Hawerchuk as their leader, but the lack of playoff success certainly wasn't his fault. In 38 post-season games with Winnipeg, Hawerchuk scored 16 goals and 49 points and remained a better than point-per-game player in the playoffs throughout his NHL career. In the final game of the 1987 Canada Cup, the line of Hawerchuk between Brent Sutter and Rick Tocchet provided the spark Canada needed to get back in the contest after falling behind 3-0. His second-period goal put Canada ahead, and even though Gretzky and Lemieux provided one of the most dramatic goals of all time to win the series, Hawerchuk was named MVP of the final game.

"We were trailing for a lot of that game, and as a line, we realized we couldn't just keep asking Gretzky and Lemieux to pull us out all the time," Hawerchuk said. "We decided we would be really aggressive, and we came right at them. That was the nature of [Sutter's and Tocchet's] games, and I was happy to follow along."

At one time, Hawerchuk seemed destined to finish his career as a Jet. However, he requested a trade in 1990, and Winnipeg was happy to comply. Both sides agreed it was time for a new start.

"I think if I had traded Dale Hawerchuk last year, I'd have had 500 people looking to string me up," said Jets GM Mike Smith at the time. "I don't get that feeling this year."

Hawerchuk didn't have much more playoff success in four-plus seasons with the Buffalo Sabres than he did in Winnipeg. He finally made it past the second round of the playoffs in his final season, advancing to the 1997 Stanley Cup final with the Philadelphia Flyers, who fell in four straight games to Detroit. Persistent back problems forced Hawerchuk out of the game that summer, with his place in the Hall of Fame assured.

– KC

Dale Hawerchuk Fast Facts

NHL career:	1981–97
Teams:	Winnipeg, Buffalo, St. Louis, Philadelphia
Post-expansion stats:	518 goals, 891 assists, 1,409 points in 1,188 games
Playoff stats:	30 goals, 69 assists, 99 points in 97 games
Individual awards: • Calder Trophy	('82)
First-team all-star berths:	0
Second-team all-star berths:	1 ('85)
Stanley Cups:	0
Legacy:	A two-way force with innate offensive instincts.

48

Pat LaFontaine

New York Dynamo

O nly the most spectacular comeback in hockey history prevented Pat LaFontaine from capturing his only NHL scoring title in 1993. With Mario Lemieux recovering from Hodgkin's disease, LaFontaine appeared headed for the Art Ross Trophy until Lemieux came back to play hours after his last radiation treatment. In the final 17 games of the season, Lemieux scored 51 points and cruised to the scoring title by 12 points over LaFontaine.

"I've always said, when a guy can come back from cancer and do what Mario did," said LaFontaine, who had 148 points in 84 games in '92–93, "that I'd be happy to lose to him any day of the week."

But exactly 10 years before Lemieux's remarkable feat, there was another battle between LaFontaine and Lemieux. And on this occasion, LaFontaine roared back to usurp Lemieux. LaFontaine was a star with the QMJHL's Verdun Jr. Canadiens, and Lemieux was tearing it up across town with the Laval Titan.

Both players were producing points at a mind-boggling rate and were filling buildings around the province of Quebec. With LaFontaine trailing Lemieux at Christmas, the Jr. Canadiens acquired Gerard Gallant and placed him on a line with LaFontaine, who hit unearthly levels and went on to score 234 points, 50 more than Lemieux.

LaFontaine spent the next 15 years of his career playing in the shadows of players like Lemieux, Wayne Gretzky and Steve Yzerman, who was selected one pick after LaFontaine in what was supposed be a mediocre 1983 draft. But while LaFontaine never gained either the individual or team accolades of Lemieux, Gretzky or Yzerman, he put together a Hall of Fame career that spanned three teams, but just one licence plate.

In the process, LaFontaine became one of the greatest American-born players in the history of the game. His roots, though, run back to Canada through his father, John, who left Tecumseh, Ont., in the 1950s with $100 in his pocket and went to school at night for eight years to gain an MBA before becoming a plant manager at Chrysler.

"Lee Iaccoca would always send him to a plant that was struggling and tell him to turn it around," LaFontaine said. "When he did, Iaccoca would send him to another one."

All the while, John LaFontaine instilled in his oldest child a deep sense of decency and integrity. On the ice, he strung lights up along the trees on Williams Lake near their home in Waterford, Mich., and taught his son how to pass and shoot. The lessons took, and LaFontaine became a minor hockey star in Michigan, scoring 324 points in his final season of midget hockey before going to Verdun. After one year of junior hockey, LaFontaine starred on the Diaper Line with Ed Olczyk and Dan Jansen on the 1984 US Olympic team and then joined the New York Islanders, who were in pursuit of their fifth straight Stanley Cup.

The Islanders were a close-knit group that, at first, looked at LaFontaine and fellow Olympian Pat Flatley as interlopers. Nothing came easily to either of them, and any respect they got from their teammates had to be earned.

> "When I look back at that [quadruple-overtime] goal [in 1987], I think that was when everything really started to come together for me."
>
> – Pat LaFontaine

"I could see where they were coming from," LaFontaine said. "If I put myself in their shoes, here's Pat Flatley and myself coming in there, and guys like Wayne Merrick, well, their jobs are on the line."

The Islanders came up short in their bid to win the Cup, losing in the final to an Edmonton Oilers team that would become a dynasty. It was the closest LaFontaine would ever come to winning a championship, though there were many moments of individual triumph with the Islanders, Buffalo Sabres and New York Rangers.

One of the most memorable came on April 18, 1987, when LaFontaine scored at 8:47 of the fourth overtime to end one of the longest playoff games in NHL history. By that time, LaFontaine had become a key player on a team that was still top-heavy with Hall of Famers.

"When I look back at that goal, I think that was when everything really started to come together for me," LaFontaine said. "I had been with the team for a couple of years, and I thought I had earned my way, but that goal really started it, and that's when I think I really came into my own and started to take off."

It was only two years later, unfortunately, that LaFontaine would sustain the first of six major concussions that ultimately ended his career. When healthy, LaFontaine continued to be one of the most offensively dynamic players in the game and was integral to Sabres' linemate Alexander Mogilny scoring 76 goals in 1992–93. But the concussions kept coming, with each one more serious than the last.

After recovering from one that wiped out most of his 1996–97 season in Buffalo, the Sabres suggested he retire. However, LaFontaine felt he could still play and was traded to the New York Rangers in September of 1997. Late in the '97–98 season, he collided violently with teammate Mike Keane; the result was his sixth concussion in seven years. With the possibility of permanent brain damage hanging over him if he sustained another concussion, LaFontaine retired.

LaFontaine went on to co-author a book titled *Companions in Courage,* about athletes who overcome a variety of obstacles; that has led to the Companions in Courage Foundation, which helps children and families facing life-threatening illnesses.

– KC

Pat LaFontaine Fast Facts

NHL career:	1984–98
Teams:	NY Islanders, Buffalo, NY Rangers
Post-expansion stats:	468 goals, 545 assists, 1,013 points in 865 games
Playoff stats:	26 goals, 36 assists, 62 points in 69 games
Individual awards: 　• **Masterton Trophy**	('95)
First-team all-star berths:	0
Second-team all-star berths:	1 ('93)
Stanley Cups:	0
Legacy:	Most purely skilled American-born NHLer.

49

Brendan Shanahan

Irish Pluck

A couple of months into Brendan Shanahan's rookie season, a veteran opponent skated into the faceoff circle and, prior to the puck being dropped, asked the kid how things were going.

"Not too great," was the reply. "Ron Hextall is tied with me in goals."

Of course, nobody had any idea that Shanahan would develop into one of the most prodigious offensive left-wingers of all time, for two reasons. First, he was playing center at the time. Second, he was one of those "character players" whose talent never quite matched his heart.

Hockey people have a mantra about the prototypical character player. It's too bad, they often say, that those guys who are so good in the dressing room insist on playing in the games as well.

Shanahan's transformation from character player to star came in the midst of the 1988–89 season, his second with the Devils. Mark Johnson went down with an injury, and Shanahan moved from third-line center to the left side on the team's top unit with Kirk Muller and John MacLean.

"In my draft year [with the OHL's London Knights], I scored 39 goals, and I was thrilled with that because I don't think I had ever scored 39 goals in a hockey season in all my life," Shanahan said. "I was a center in junior, and I was more of a passer than a finisher. I got into the NHL, and I realized that I was a better winger and I was actually a better left-winger. It was like overnight, all of a sudden that was it. Some people say it's gradual, but for me it was overnight."

And he has been scoring ever since, at a clip that will likely put him at No. 2 on the all time goals and points list for left-wingers, behind Luc Robitaille. He remains the only player in NHL history to score 600 goals and 1,200 points while accumulating more than 2,000 penalty minutes. Including the 2006–07 season, Shanahan had fewer than 100 PIM in a season only twice and was an integral part of the 1987 Canadian world junior team that was ejected from the tournament – along with the Soviet Union – after a spectacular brawl.

"I came in and fought a lot, earned some space and some respect on the ice," Shanahan said. "It wasn't just fighting, it was the type of players I was fighting against. It was [Rick] Tocchet, it was [Willi] Plett, [Craig] Berube and guys like that."

Shanahan has never been reticent to drop his gloves, but he inflicts the most damage on opponents when he stays on the ice. In New Jersey, he was more of a typical power forward and scored most of his goals from just outside the crease. But by the time he moved on to the St. Louis Blues in 1991, he had diversified his game and developed a lethal wrist shot that made him a far more dangerous offensive player.

And while Shanahan's hockey exploits could fill entire volumes, that's only part of what has made him such a memorable character in the game's history. Over the course of his career, he has been a constant source of memorable one-line witticisms. What else could you expect from a man who kissed the Blarney Stone in Ireland when he visited the country as a teenager?

> **"I came in and fought a lot, earned some space and some respect on the ice."**
>
> **– Brendan Shanahan**

Among his off-season activities – according to his teams' media guides, at least – Shanahan has played goal for the Irish national soccer team and spent one off-season playing saxophone in a jazz band. When asked by a reporter to display his musical talents, Shanahan replied, "Sorry, no sax on game days."

Shanahan also has been involved in some of the most controversial transactions in NHL history. When he signed with the Blues in the summer of 1991 as a restricted free agent, the Devils were awarded Scott Stevens as compensation (and while Stevens was originally horrified at going to the Devils, he led them to three Stanley cups). And, in the summer of 1995, Blues GM Mike Keenan traded Shanahan to Hartford for Chris Pronger, a mistake-prone youngster who would develop into one of the game's best defensemen.

Shanahan was never comfortable with the Whalers. The day he was dealt there, he received a phone message from a former teammate saying, "Look at the bright side: No more road trips to Hartford." Early in his second season with the Whalers, Shanahan demanded a trade and was dealt to Detroit for Keith Primeau, Paul Coffey and the Red Wings' first-round draft choice.

He went on to win three Stanley cups in Detroit and solidified his Hall of Fame credentials before signing with the New York Rangers in 2006.

But it was during the lockout that Shanahan made what might be his most indelible mark on the game. He convened a hockey summit aimed at ridding the game of the obstruction that had slowed the NHL to a crawl, then was an integral part of the rules committee that ushered in a new, offense-friendly league.

"I've said it lots of times, when Michael Jordan is going up for a jump shot, defensive players aren't allowed to grab him by his hips and haul him down," Shanahan said. "That's kind of where the NHL had gotten to over the course of several years."

– KC

Brendan Shanahan Fast Facts

NHL career:	1987–2007 (active)
Teams:	New Jersey, St. Louis, Hartford, Detroit, NY Rangers
Post-expansion stats:	627 goals, 667 assists, 1,294 points in 1,417 games
Playoff stats:	58 goals, 68 assists, 126 points in 167 games
Individual awards: • **Clancy Memorial Trophy**	('03)
First-team all-star berths:	2 ('94, '00)
Second-team all-star berths:	1 ('02)
Stanley Cups:	3
Legacy:	Power forward provides goals, sweat and swagger.

50

Rob Blake

King of Defense

Ken Gratton saw something in the skinny, lanky kid playing defense for the Simcoe, Ont., minor midgets, so he asked the young man and his father whether they would attend the tryouts for his Jr. B team the next season.

"We didn't know anything about how hockey worked," said the skinny, lanky defenseman. "But we figured we would go there and give it a try."

That player was Robert Bowlby Blake, and so began his unlikely and mercurial trajectory toward NHL stardom. But the story has an interesting twist. Gratton's son, Dan, was selected 10th overall by the Los Angeles Kings that summer, and the enigmatic young man seemed destined for stardom. But not Ken Gratton, not anybody, could ever convince Dan to take hockey and training and off-ice lifestyle seriously enough. He played just seven games with the Kings and was a first-round flop.

But Blake, he was different. Ken Gratton was able to convince Blake to use his size to his advantage to punish people. He saw in Blake an above-average skater and realized Blake could become a devastating open-ice hitter. Blake listened and learned – and earned his first calling card in hockey on the strength of his physical play.

The skill, poise and maturation would come a little later, and when Blake learned to put it all together, he had an array of skills that would make him a Norris Trophy winner and Stanley Cup champion.

All that from the humble beginnings in Simcoe, a town of 16,000 on the shores of Lake Erie just south of Hamilton. The town that produced Red Kelly would later churn out an assembly line of NHL players in Blake, Dwayne Roloson, Jassen Cullimore and Ryan VandenBussche. Rick Kowalsky, another native of Simcoe, was the captain of the OHL's Sault Ste. Marie Greyhounds when they won the Memorial Cup in 1993.

"For a span of about six years, they were producing quite a few NHLers for a place so small," Blake said. "The funny thing is, we all grew up about five minutes from each other."

Five years after leaving Simcoe, Blake found himself in the NHL without ever playing a game in the minors. His skills, which improved in Ontario Jr. B with Brantford and later the legendary Stratford Cullitons, were refined over three years at Bowling Green University. With four games remaining in the 1989–90 season, Blake was lured out of school and signed by the Kings.

It's almost the same path that was followed by Jack Johnson, who joined the Kings at the end of the 2006–07 season. The Kings re-signed Blake in the summer of 2006, in part so he could mentor their future young star – the same way Larry Robinson did for Blake when Blake broke into the league.

It wasn't long before Blake was making an impact in Los Angeles. With just four NHL regular season games under his belt, he had proven himself enough to dress in eight of the Kings' 10 games in the 1990 playoffs. Blake had scored 23 goals and 59 points that season with Bowling Green and found his offensive stride with the Kings, who were among the last great offensive teams of the 1990s. Those teams were led by Wayne Gretzky, who helped transform Blake from an offensive college defenseman to an offensive weapon in the NHL. Of the 12 goals he scored in his first full season with the Kings, nine came on the power play and largely were the end result of Gretzky's creativity.

> "I could always shoot the puck, and when you're playing up top on the power play and the greatest player ever is feeding you the puck, it's a pretty good situation."
>
> **– Rob Blake**

"I think having the opportunity to play right away was huge for my development," Blake said. "I could always shoot the puck, and when you're playing up top on the power play and the greatest player ever is feeding you the puck, it's a pretty good situation. I was always able to skate, and in the late 1980s and early 1990s, if you could skate, there were holes you could find for open ice."

Blake found himself in another great situation in 2001 when the Kings, who were unable to sign him to a contract extension, dealt him to the Colorado Avalanche at the trade deadline. The deal, which worked out well for both sides – the Kings received Adam Deadmarsh and Aaron Miller in return – remains one of the most significant ever made at the deadline. Blake went on to win the Stanley Cup that year with Colorado and was a major contributor, playing almost 30 minutes a game and scoring six goals and 19 points in 23 games.

Blake's most gratifying individual season, though, was in 1997–98, when he won his only Norris Trophy over finalists Chris Pronger and Nicklas Lidstrom. Blake won the award on the strength of a late-season charge on a weak Kings team. He was minus-3 that season and has been a minus player several times (he was minus-26 in 2006–07), largely because he has handled much of the workload on some bad teams. Even as a 37-year-old in 2006–07, he was playing 26 minutes a game.

"I remember the year I won the Norris, for the first 20 games of the season, nothing was going right for me," Blake said. "I didn't even make it to the all-star game that year. I knew I was doing something wrong, and that was a real wakeup call for me. I really put it together, and things seemed to fall into place."

– KC

Rob Blake Fast Facts

NHL career:	1990–2007 (active)
Teams:	Los Angeles, Colorado
Post-expansion stats:	214 goals, 457 assists, 671 points in 1,056 games
Playoff stats:	24 goals, 43 assists, 67 points in 125 games
Individual awards: • **Norris Trophy**	('98)
First-team all-star berths:	1 ('98)
Second-team all-star berths:	3 ('00, '01, '02)
Stanley Cups:	1
Legacy:	The best defenseman in Kings' history.

51

Luc Robitaille

Goal Miner

When the Los Angeles Kings retired Luc Robitaille's No. 20 in 2007, they held a dinner in his honor. At one point during the festivities, Kings GM Dean Lombardi produced a scouting report he had prepared on Robitaille back in 1984.

"Great hands, terrible skater." Prospects of having a significant career in the NHL: not exactly zero, but you could see it from where Lombardi was standing.

So it was only fitting the son of a Montreal scrap yard owner was in the scrap heap of the 1984 draft.

Lombardi was hardly a lone voice in the wilderness, considering the Kings took Robitaille 171st overall in that draft, 102 picks after they selected baseball pitcher Tom Glavine. But had the Kings simply selected Robitaille with their first-round pick and then packed up their things and gone home, they would have been just as productive.

Consider that when Robitaille retired after the 2005–06 season, no left-winger in the history of the game has scored as many goals (668) or earned as many points (1,394), or scored as many goals (63) or points (125) in a single season.

Of the 11 other players the Kings chose in 1984, three of them played in the NHL and combined for 21 goals and 100 points in 242 games. In fact, including that 1984 crop, you have to go all the way to the 70th overall pick of the 1988 draft – when the Kings selected Rob Blake – to find enough players to match Robitaille's career point total. (That's 46 players, in case you were thinking of looking it up.)

But the funny thing is that while Robitaille continued to prove his doubters wrong, the knocks on him never let up, even after he won the Calder Trophy as the league's top rookie in 1987. The next season, in the midst of a 53-goal sophomore campaign, Robitaille played in his first all-star game after being voted to the Campbell Conference starting lineup.

This was back when the players and coaches actually cared about the result of the all-star game. And, it was back when Robitaille's talent garnered little respect. As he was about to join all-star linemates Wayne Gretzky and Mark Messier on the ice, Robitaille remembers being stunned by Campbell coach Glen Sather.

"He said to me, 'As soon as they drop the puck, you come back to the bench because I'm going to put someone else out there,' " Robitaille said. "And I'm like, 'What are you talking about? I got voted into the game!' "

When Robitaille was playing junior for a Hull Olympiques team coached by Pat Burns and owned by Gretzky, someone once wrote that he skated slower than a Zamboni. Robitaille simply used those kinds of words to fuel a passion that propelled those legs to go straight to the net and the hands to find the back of it with the puck.

"I had a lot of fun sticking it to some people," Robitaille said. "But it was never about that. It was always about playing a game I loved and playing it with passion."

> "It was always about playing a game I loved and playing it with passion."
>
> – Luc Robitaille

Robitaille showed up in Los Angeles unable to speak any English and learned the language by watching *Three's Company* and *The Flintstones.* He arrived two years pre-Gretzky as the Kings were putting together a formidable group of youngsters. Among them was Jimmy Carson, who was taken second overall in 1986 and scored 37 goals as a rookie in 1987, eight fewer than Robitaille. Carson was the centerpiece in the package for Gretzky but was never the same player after the 1988 trade. Meanwhile, the closest the Kings ever came to a Stanley Cup was losing in the final to the Montreal Canadiens in 1993.

Robitaille had two more tours of duty with the Kings before retiring and managed to win a Stanley Cup with the Detroit Red Wings in 2002. He wasn't a front-line player for the Wings by that point in his career – at least, not like he was in 1994 when he led Canada to its first World Championship in 33 years in Italy.

Canada had not won the tournament since the Trail (BC) Smoke Eaters did it in 1961. With Robitaille as captain, Canada defeated Finland in the gold medal game. It was a perfect ending, with Robitaille scoring the winner in the shootout.

"I'll always be proud of that," he said. "Glen Sather made me captain of that team and told me he wanted me to be the leader. During that game, I was thinking, 'Who knows? This might be my only chance to win something.' "

– KC

Luc Robitaille Fast Facts

NHL career:	1986–2006
Teams:	Los Angeles, Pittsburgh, NY Rangers, Detroit
Post-expansion stats:	668 goals, 726 assists, 1,394 points in 1,431 games
Playoff stats:	58 goals, 69 assists, 127 points in 159 games
Individual awards: • Calder Trophy	('87)
First-team all-star berths:	5 ('88, '89, '90, '91, '93)
Second-team all-star berths:	3 ('87, '92, '01)
Stanley Cups:	1
Legacy:	Knocked for his skating but never for his scoring.

Stan Mikita

Blackhawk Born Again

By the time the first wave of expansion had hit the NHL, Stan Mikita was in the midst of a remarkable transformation. With one Lady Byng Trophy already to his credit, Mikita would win another in the first year of the expanded league, thus completing his startling metamorphosis from angry ruffian to skilled gentleman.

Mikita loves to tell the story of his epiphany and has told it many times in many forms. The way Mikita tells it, he arrived home from a road trip one day and was greeted at the door by his young daughter.

"She said to me, 'I watched you last night, and you were really good,' and I said, 'Well, thank you, dear,' " Mikita recalled. "Then she asked me, 'When that man with the stripes on his sweater blew the whistle, why did Uncle Bobby and Uncle Kenny go one way, and you went the other way and sat down all by yourself? Were you being a bad boy?' That really made me think."

While Mikita was thinking, he knew he was smart enough to change his game for the better. After all, he was once a kid who arrived in Canada from Czechoslovakia at the age of eight and couldn't speak a word of English, yet within six months had mastered the language and been promoted to Grade 4.

But as a young man he was also taunted by other children and was referred to as a "DP", or Displaced Person, one of the most derogatory racial insults someone could receive in the late 1940s. That, in part, fuelled the rage that made the 5 foot 9, 160-pounder such a feared opponent on the ice.

Ed Belfour

Aggressive Eagle

Long before he first tended goal in the NHL and long after he backstopped the Dallas Stars to a Stanley Cup in 1999, Ed Belfour has had to deal with doubters. And he has made a masterful career out of showing them the light.

"There's always that good feeling showing people they were wrong about you," Belfour told *The Hockey News* in 2003. "I've been in a position for a long time where people want to knock you down, where they think you're not as good as what your achievements show. By no means am I a braggart, but sure, it's nice to prove the doubters wrong."

The recipient of two Vezina trophies and a Calder Trophy, Belfour wasn't given much of a chance to make the NHL in the first place. For starters, the Carmen, Man., native played Manitoba Jr. A until he was 21, before transferring to the University of North Dakota for the 1986–87 season.

It was in the NCAA that Belfour began to show the technique and attention to detail for which he would eventually be renowned. By the end of the year, he had a 29-4 record and a stingy 2.37 goals-against average – and led his schoolmates to an NCAA championship.

> **"I'm sure many people don't realize there is a very kind man beneath the [goalie] mask."**
>
> **– Vladislav Tretiak**

The NHL soon took note, and Chicago signed Belfour as a free agent in 1987.

"He has quickness and the ability to recover," said Hawks scouting director Jack Davison at the time. "He's a standup goaltender who can challenge the shooter."

There was something else that stood out about Belfour: his temper.

"You'd better not fool around in front of his net," Davison said, "or he'll move you out of there himself."

Belfour never denied his dislike for opposing forwards who crowded his crease.

"I think I'm an aggressive goaltender," he said. "I get involved in the game. If someone is in the crease in front of me and blocks my view, it doesn't bother me that I clear the way for myself sometimes."

After apprenticing for three years in the International League and on the Canadian national team, Belfour earned full-time NHL employment in 1990–91 and went 43-19-7 with a 2.47 GAA for Chicago.

His efforts that season earned Belfour rookie-of-the-year honors, his first of two Vezina trophies as the league's top goalie, his first of four Jennings trophies for fewest goals allowed and a nomination for the Hart Trophy.

In 1991–92, Belfour won 12 straight playoff games for the Blackhawks before Chicago was swept by Mario Lemieux's Pittsburgh Penguins in the Stanley Cup final. The next season, he won his second Vezina.

Somehow, though, Belfour never seemed to have the full backing of team management. He often clashed with Hawks' coach Mike Keenan in the early days and with backup goalie Jeff Hackett toward the end of his stint in Chicago.

When Belfour was dealt to San Jose late in the '96–97 season, he was having a rough year on the stats sheet. So, after he continued to struggle in the 13 games he played for the Sharks, Belfour's doubters reappeared and cranked up the volume again.

Undeterred, Belfour signed as a free agent with the Dallas Stars in the summer of 1997 – and the payoff began immediately. He led the team to its first Presidents' Trophy while posting a 1.88 GAA and 37-12-10 regular-season record.

The Stars were eliminated by Detroit in the Western Conference final that spring, but Dallas stuck with Belfour the next season. He rewarded them with 35 more wins, another sub-2.00 GAA (1.99, to be precise) and another Presidents' Trophy.

Belfour, though, was at a stage in his career where he needed to augment his regular season success with post-season accolades. He rose to the occasion in the 1999 playoffs, going 16-7 with three shutouts and a 1.67 GAA to power the Stars to their first championship in franchise history.

"I'll tell you, Eddie Belfour was unbelievable for us that year," said Stars teammate Joe Nieuwendyk, who took on and defeated future Hall of Famers Grant Fuhr, Patrick Roy and Dominik Hasek during the '99 playoffs. "He brought us so much confidence. Just a professional, through and through."

Over the years, Belfour's temper occasionally manifested itself in brushes with the law. In 2000, he plead guilty to a misdemeanor charge of resisting arrest after a physical confrontation with a security guard at a Dallas hotel; and twice during the 2006–07 season, he was involved in incidents where police were called to the scene of Long Island and Miami-area bars to deal with an unruly Belfour.

That said, those who know him best say Belfour is misunderstood.

"I'm sure many people don't realize there is a very kind man beneath the [goalie] mask," said legendary Russian goalie Vladislav Tretiak, who mentored Belfour in Chicago. The pair remained friends. "Sometimes he is rough around the edges and historically has not been very friendly with the media, but that is only on the surface. Inside, Eddie is a very gentle man."

The Stars cut Belfour loose after the '01–02 campaign, but he signed a three-year deal with Toronto, where he set a personal best for shutouts in a single season (10) and passed his boyhood idol Tony Esposito, as well as Glenn Hall and Jacques Plante, to move into second place on the NHL's all-time win list.

After three seasons, Belfour's option year in Toronto was not picked up. So, as he approached age 42 – and despite battling back problems for much of his career – the former triathlete signed on to play with the Florida Panthers in 2006–07.

With age, Belfour admitted, one's legacy does spring to mind a little more often. And he's proud of his.

"Sometimes somebody will show me something, or I'll happen to come across a stat, and as you get older you start understanding more about that aspect of the game," he said. "But I'd rather be remembered as a fierce competitor and as a great teammate than for any one thing I've done."

– AP

Ed Belfour Fast Facts

NHL career:	1988–2007 (active)
Teams:	Chicago, San Jose, Dallas, Toronto, Florida
Post-expansion stats:	484-320-111 record, 2.50 GAA, 76 shutouts in 963 games
Playoff stats:	88-68 record, 2.17 GAA, 14 shutouts in 161 games
Individual awards:	
• Calder Trophy	('91)
• Vezina Trophy	('91, '93)
• Jennings Trophy	('91, '93, '95, '99)
First-team all-star berths:	2 ('91, '93)
Second-team all-star berths:	1 ('95)
Stanley Cups:	1
Legacy:	Superb positional goalie played at elite level into his 40s.

54

Yvan Cournoyer

Speed to Burn

Serving as captain of the Montreal Canadiens requires shoulders broad enough to bear the weight of millions of expectations. And though he measured in at only 5 foot 7, Yvan Cournoyer's inner strength made him one of the best-ever Habs captains.

"When I was a youngster I always dreamed of playing for the Canadiens," said Cournoyer, who won an astounding 10 Stanley cups in his 15-year career. "But, as everyone else has learned playing for Montreal, you've got to be good all the time. If not, there always seems to be someone there to replace you. Each year we had to be No. 1. There was nothing else."

A product of the Canadiens' junior system, Cournoyer – nicknamed The Roadrunner for his scorching speed – began his NHL career in 1964–65 and soon was known for the quick, heavy wrist shot he developed by practicing with a four-pound lead puck.

For the first few seasons, his ice time was limited to mostly power play minutes on a deep, talented Montreal team. But in the post-expansion NHL, Cournoyer's opportunities grew – and so did his job description. In 1968–69, he exploded for 43 goals and a career-best 87 points in 76 games, while helping the Habs to their fourth Stanley Cup in five seasons.

Like many dynasties, Cournoyer said, the Canadiens were successful in large part because of the family-like atmosphere.

"We were a very close-knit team," the Drummondville, Que., native told *The Hockey News* in 1979. "There was no French or English. When we lost, we lost together. When we won, we won together."

While he always focused on improving his all-around game, Cournoyer was renowned for his offense. He had a career-high 47 goals in 1971–72, and at the 1972 Summit Series, he scored the winning goal in Game 2 and game-tying goal in Game 8 for Canada, while finishing the tournament with three goals and five points in eight games.

Cournoyer carried that momentum into the 1972–73 NHL campaign and delivered the greatest year of his career. After notching 40 goals and 79 points in 67 games – and finishing the season an amazing plus-50 – he scored 15 goals and 25 points in 17 games to win his sixth Cup.

For his contributions that spring, Cournoyer was awarded the Conn Smythe Trophy as playoff MVP. But perhaps the greatest honor he would ever receive in the NHL was yet to come.

When Henri Richard retired from the Canadiens in 1975, the team needed a new captain. And though he was a robust 32 years of age and headed toward the twilight in his career, Cournoyer was unanimously selected by his teammates to replace Richard and don the *C*.

"I never dreamed of being captain of the Canadiens," he said. "It was an honor to be following in the same footsteps as former captains like Henri Richard and Jean Beliveau."

> **"There was no French or English. When we lost, we lost together. When we won, we won together."**
>
> **– Yvan Cournoyer**

The 1976–77 campaign saw back problems start to take a toll on Cournoyer, and the always tough Montreal media was right on top of him, questioning whether he had lost a step. He played through the pain and managed 53 points in 60 games, but required season-ending surgery that caused him to miss the Habs' second consecutive Cup-winning post-season.

Cournoyer returned to the Canadiens' lineup for the 1977–78 season and found a way to fight through the increasingly agonizing back woes. It would be his last full year, but he gutted out 24 goals and 53 points, and added seven goals and 11 points in the playoffs to pace Montreal to its third straight Cup.

At age 35, Cournoyer intended to continue to play for the Habs. However, after 15 games in '78–79, another back operation forced him to the sidelines for good. "It came as quite a shock to me when it happened," said Cournoyer, who was diagnosed with a serious disc injury. "I thought it was nothing more than a pulled muscle at first. So I continued playing despite the pain. But the pain continued, and [after] another examination was taken, the disc problem was discovered."

Just like that, he was no longer allowed to play the game he had adored since childhood. And the adjustment was not an easy one for him.

"I had very bad feelings when I retired from hockey," he said. "After all, hockey had been my whole life, and then it was over, all too quickly."

Despite its abrupt ending, Cournoyer's career was superb enough to land him in the Hall of Fame in 1982.

Looking back on his career, Cournoyer said he didn't ask to have those millions of expectations placed upon him and his teammates. But he knows that, in meeting or exceeding those lofty demands so many times in Montreal, he earned himself a lasting legacy in the team's storied history.

"There is a lot of pressure being a Canadien," Cournoyer said. "But I enjoyed the pressure of playing in Montreal. I think it helped mold me as a person."

– AP

Yvan Cournoyer Fast Facts*

NHL career:	1963–79
Teams:	Montreal
Post-expansion stats:	374 goals, 399 assists, 773 points in 774 games
Playoff stats:	51 goals, 48 assists, 99 points in 102 games
Individual awards: • **Conn Smythe Trophy**	('73)
First-team all-star berths:	0
Second-team all-star berths:	4 ('69, '71, '72, '73)
Stanley Cups:	8
Legacy:	They didn't come any faster than this heart-and-soul Hab.

*Fast Facts does not include any pre-expansion statistics or information.

55

Glenn Anderson

Big-Game Hunter

The hockey that was played at the 1980 Olympics made household names out of the US men's team. But it also was a seminal moment in the soon-to-bud NHL career of future star Glenn Anderson.

"It was one of the biggest stepping stones in my career, both in terms of developing into a player and developing into a human being," said Anderson, a member of the Canadian team that finished sixth at Lake Placid, NY "I got my very first taste of losing and what it felt like to lose, and I never wanted to have that happen again.

"As soon as I turned pro, it was like I had to treat each game as if it were my last shot."

Anderson, a six-time Stanley Cup champion with the Oilers and Rangers, also learned the value of conditioning at a time when off-ice physical fitness was under-appreciated.

"In the Olympics, you really learned how to train and become an athlete," Anderson said. "At that time, Olympic athletes and professional athletes were two very different things. We were on the ice for three or four hours a day, and then you had three or four hours of dryland training.

"So when I walked into the dressing room of a professional team, I looked around and thought, 'Oh my god, You guys have got to be kidding me.' It was like night and day from where I just came from."

Though Anderson understood the team-first nature of hockey, it was clear he was a breed apart from the typical NHLer. Even before his amateur career began at the University of Denver, the Vancouver native saw life – and hockey – in his own unique way.

"The NHL wasn't my No. 1 goal or ambition," said Anderson, who as a child was a fan of Russian star forward Alexander Yakushev. "I got a taste of good coaching and life philosophy going back to the University of Denver and having [hockey pioneer] Father [David] Bauer as a mentor in my life. That opened me up to more worldly things, and not just the NHL. So my goal was to play internationally before it was to play in the NHL."

Selected by the Oilers 69th overall in the 1979 draft, Anderson played 11 seasons in his first stint with Edmonton and won five Cups as part of a star-studded lineup. One of the most colorful Oilers, he was criticized for perceived eccentricities by some. But he was always comfortable in his own skin, even if others weren't.

"I know the type of person I am," Anderson said. "You knew that when you'd go to leadership camps and they split you into different categories. There weren't too many people in my category… and they were usually goalies."

While an Oiler, he hit the 50-goal plateau twice and had three seasons of more than 100 points. Anderson's greatest glories, though, came in the post-season.

When the games mattered most, Anderson was Captain Clutch. His five career playoff overtime goals are the third-most in league history – behind only Joe Sakic and Maurice Richard – and his 17 game-winning goals in the playoffs rank fifth on the NHL's all-time list.

Interestingly, Anderson counts not the championships he won but his experiences on the losing side of the ledger as his most meaningful moments in the game.

> "There weren't too many people in my category… and they were usually goalies."
>
> – Glenn Anderson

"Before you can win, you have to lose," he said. "My learning experiences are probably my fondest. The '80 Olympics was a big standout. The Miracle on Manchester, when [the Oilers] were winning 5-0 and [the Kings] came back to win 6-5 in overtime after Darryl Evans scored over Grant Fuhr's shoulder.

"Those are standouts in my mind, and I'll remember those games forever, because those are the ones you learn from. If you're constantly winning, you don't appreciate it if you haven't lost before."

Along with Fuhr, Anderson was dealt in 1991 to Toronto, where he played two-plus seasons and helped bring the Leafs within a goal of the Stanley Cup final in 1993.

For someone who was used to the selflessness of the Oilers' organization, helping turn the previously sad-sack Maple Leafs into Cup contenders was no small feat.

"I went from one of the best dressing rooms to one of the worst dressing rooms," he said. "There were key players on that team who had to be eliminated or turned. So you try and turn them first, and if you can't, you get rid of them. You can't win without everybody tugging on the rope at the same time."

Toronto dealt Anderson to the Rangers at the trade deadline in 1994, and he arrived in New York just in time to help the Blueshirts break a 54-year Cup drought.

"[The trade] worked out good for me," said Anderson with a chuckle. "In '93, they gave us a ring and a parade [in Toronto] for [the Leafs] winning the division. And the next year, I win the Cup and have a parade in Manhattan. Two parades and two rings in two years, but only one Cup!"

Anderson finished his NHL career with two short stints in St. Louis as well as a brief return to Edmonton. He also fulfilled a longtime wish and traveled the world as a player, skating for Finnish, German, Swiss and Italian teams before retiring in 1997.

"When you signed with Edmonton, [coach Glen Sather] gave you a psychology test, and you were asked your goals and ambitions," he said. "And mine was playing hockey and visiting different countries, whereas everyone else's was hoisting the Stanley Cup over their heads."

– AP

Glenn Anderson Fast Facts

NHL career:	1980–96
Teams:	Edmonton, Toronto, New York Rangers, St. Louis
Post-expansion stats:	498 goals, 601 assists, 1,099 points in 1,129 games
Playoff stats:	93 goals, 121 assists, 214 points in 225 games
Individual awards:	None
First-team all-star berths:	0
Second-team all-star berths:	0
Stanley Cups:	6
Legacy:	Saved his net-driving, goal-scoring best for the post-season.

56

Denis Savard

The Spin Master

Denis Savard began his Hall of Fame career in the working-class Montreal suburb of Verdun, where his mother and father operated a small grocery store, a *depanneur,* not far from the arena that now bears his name.

As a talented young player, Savard had two close friends with uncanny similarities. One was Denis Cyr, the other was Denis Tremblay; remarkably, all three shared the same birth date, Feb. 4, 1961, as well as a first name. Fans dubbed them Les Trois Denis as they filled the net as linemates in minor hockey, and later with the QMJHL's Verdun Jr. Canadiens.

All three dreamed of one day starring for their beloved Montreal Canadiens, and that's just what the Habs needed, a few more potential Francophone superstars. But the dream was much more realistic for Savard than it was for the other two. The Canadiens held the first overall selection in 1980, and Savard was theirs for the taking. But GM Irving Grundman instead took Doug Wickenheiser, a big power forward from the WHL's Regina Pats who was three inches taller and 40 pounds heavier than Savard.

Chicago nabbed Savard with the third overall pick, and the young center quickly showed off his self-confidence, boldly stating after the draft: "When the season starts, I'm going to prove I'm better than Wickenheiser."

The decision to select Wickenheiser was criticized in Montreal, and Savard went about proving himself right immediately. In his first game with Chicago in 1980–81, he had three assists; in his first road game, with Wickenheiser looking on as a healthy scratch, Savard scored a goal and added two assists against the Canadiens and was selected the game's first star.

While Wickenheiser constantly struggled to live up to expectations, Savard spent most of the next 17 years dazzling hockey fans with an arsenal of skills, skating and puck-possession abilities. Savard scored countless truly breathtaking goals with the Blackhawks, darting in and out among players until the perfect chance to shoot presented itself, with the puck attached to his stick as though tied there by string.

At his best, Savard didn't simply score goals. He created works of art.

"For me, it wasn't about trying to please the fans or anything like that, it was just, 'Hey, this is how I play,' " Savard said. "I always thought when I was playing that I never wanted to show the same thing every time and try to keep people off their guard. And I was always taught to protect the puck. If you're facing an opponent when you have the puck, it's easier for them to take it away from you. That's why I did that spin a lot."

Many in Chicago credited him with inventing the Savardian Spinarama, but it was another Savard who both invented and perfected the move. Serge Savard (no relation) – who, as the Habs' GM, traded Chris Chelios to bring Denis Savard to the Canadiens in 1990 – used the move to avoid oncoming checkers. But while Serge Savard employed it very deliberately and used a long, loping stride, Denis Savard electrified fans by being able to complete the 360-degree turn at full speed, all the while cradling the puck on his stick and leaving defenders spinning in his wake.

When Savard left for his first training camp in Chicago, he spoke almost no English. Before he departed, he told his father he wouldn't be coming back and that he would make the team. It may have sounded like bravado at the time, but Savard said it was his way of dealing with the pressure of making it to the NHL.

> **"If you're facing an opponent when you have the puck, it's easier for them to take it away from you. That's why I did that spin a lot."**
>
> **– Denis Savard**

"My parents, they would work 14 or 16 hours a day, until 10 o'clock, and they did this every night for a long time," Savard said. "The biggest thing for me was I didn't want to disappoint anybody. I had two older brothers [Andre and Luc] who played and didn't make it to the NHL, so I was thinking that I was the one who had to get it done."

Savard got it done, all right. He was the centerpiece on some great Blackhawk teams that suffered the misfortune of being not quite as dynamic and explosive as the Edmonton Oilers in the 1980s. It seemed that Savard would fall victim, as many players do, to bad timing, until he was traded to the Canadiens in the twilight of his career.

Three years after his trade to Montreal, the Canadiens won the 1993 Stanley Cup behind the brilliant goaltending of Patrick Roy and 10 overtime victories. Savard injured his foot in the second round and missed the entire final, but the moment captain Guy Carbonneau accepted the Cup, he passed it on to Savard, who by that time was acting as a quasi-assistant coach to Jacques Demers.

From there, Savard moved on to a brief stint with the woeful Tampa Bay Lightning, before playing out the final two-plus seasons of his career in Chicago, where it all started.

In the end, Savard never had a 50-goal season, never won a major individual award and never was on a first all-star team. But he played with such flair and artistry that he will never be forgotten.

"Sometimes I think about what would have happened if Montreal drafted me," Savard said. "They had a great team, and I probably would have played with Guy [Lafleur] and that would have been all right too. But I think things turned out pretty well here too."

– KC

Denis Savard Fast Facts

NHL career:	1980–97
Teams:	Chicago, Montreal, Tampa Bay
Post-expansion stats:	473 goals, 865 assists, 1,338 points in 1,196 games
Playoff stats:	66 goals, 109 assists, 175 points in 169 games
Individual awards:	None
First-team all-star berths:	0
Second-team all-star berths:	1 ('83)
Stanley Cups:	1
Legacy:	Skating, stickhandling and playmaking skills were unsurpassed.

57

Sidney Crosby

The Future

Like Wayne Gretzky, Sidney Crosby was a hockey prodigy from his earliest days. And like The Great One, in many ways, hockey has been all he has known, all his life.

That explains why Crosby treats each game as if it is the only thing in the world that matters.

"My parents always told me when you do something, you do it to your full potential," said Crosby, the Pittsburgh Penguins' legend-in-the-making. "They said, basically, don't cut corners. That is what I have tried to do, and I have been fortunate enough to have good stuff happen so far."

Good stuff. That's one way to put it.

Others would put it this way: Before he played his first NHL game in 2005, Crosby had amassed 183 assists and 303 points in two seasons with the QMJHL's Rimouski Oceanic. He was the Canadian Hockey League's rookie of the year in 2004 and collected back-to-back player-of-the-year awards in 2004 and '05.

Hype surrounded Crosby as the 2005 NHL entry draft drew near, but he had grown accustomed to it years before. The son of former Canadiens' goaltending prospect Troy Crosby, Sidney had given his first interview at age 7. The Oceanic made him the No. 1 pick in the QMJHL midget draft. And Gretzky himself said that if anyone could break his NHL scoring records, it was the Cole Harbour, NS, native.

So when the NHL organized a media blitz around the draft lottery that would award Pittsburgh the right to select Crosby first overall, nobody was surprised. Sid the Kid was the latest in a long line of "next ones" that the hockey world expected to mirror or better Gretzky.

Two years in, Crosby had disappointed no one.

His rookie season afforded him the opportunity to play with Penguins owner/legend Mario Lemieux before he retired, and Crosby finished the 2005–06 campaign with 63 assists and 102 points in 81 games.

The biggest challenge, the 18-year-old said, was the increased flow of the game.

"For me, [the toughest adjustment] had to do with how quickly things happen out there," said Crosby in the summer of 2006. "You're playing with guys who've been doing it for so long, and they're smart at what they do, so you have to make sure you make quick decisions, because everyone out there is smart and quick too. You have to think fast on your feet."

The youngest NHLer to reach the 100-point plateau, Crosby also had 110 penalty minutes in his first season, indicative of a style that didn't shy away from physical contact. In fact, he thrived on it.

"Aside from the great talent he possesses, the thing that distances him from the other great players in the league is his competitiveness," said veteran star Brendan Shanahan. "We have so many great players who have amazing talent, but what Sidney has is second, third and fourth effort. He refuses to be denied.

> "People used to describe what made Wayne Gretzky and Mario Lemieux so great, and it was that same competitiveness that Sidney has."
>
> – Brendan Shanahan

"People used to describe what made Wayne Gretzky and Mario Lemieux so great, and it was that same competitiveness that Sidney has."

Crosby finished second to 19-year-old Washington Capitals phenom Alexander Ovechkin in rookie-of-the-year balloting, but the 2006–07 sophomore of the year was no contest. Midway through the season, a THN poll of NHLers pegged Crosby as the game's best player. And by the end of the campaign, he had powered the Pens to their first playoff berth since 2001, captured the Art Ross Trophy with 120 points in 79 games and taken home both the Pearson Award and Hart Trophy as NHL MVP.

"It is amazing," said Penguins GM Ray Shero of Crosby's ascendancy to the top of the league. "Through the course of a game, Sidney will do something where you think you'd already seen everything, and he manages to come up with something new. He'll do something, and I'll turn to [senior Penguins adviser] Eddie Johnston and say, 'Did you see that?'"

"To sit there and watch him in a game is one thing... But to be able to watch him practise is unreal. He's an incredible practise player. He makes himself better in practise. He challenges himself."

Added Tampa Bay Lightning star Martin St-Louis: "[Crosby is] obviously the real deal. He's so mature for his age. He sure doesn't look like a 19-year-old out there, the way he skates and controls games... the way he makes things happen... He is the type of player you want to build a team around."

With so stunning an NHL debut, Crosby has the weight of an entire league on his shoulders. He's the NHL's poster boy for years to come – but, like many of the legendarily modest all-time greats of the game, he doesn't worry about fulfilling the wishes of others.

"I have my own expectations," Crosby said. "I think I always set my standards high. Whether I've met the expectations of people around the game, I'll leave that for them to decide."

– AP

Sidney Crosby Fast Facts

NHL career:	2005–07 (active)
Teams:	Pittsburgh
Post-expansion stats:	75 goals, 147 assists, 222 points in 160 games
Playoff stats:	3 goals, 2 assists, 5 points in 5 games
Individual awards:	
• Hart Trophy	('07)
• Art Ross Trophy	('07)
• Pearson Award	('07)
First-team all-star berths:	1
Second-team all-star berths:	0
Stanley Cups:	0
Legacy:	"The Next One" has arrived. Enjoy.

58

Darryl Sittler

10-Point Player

As the third-oldest sibling in a family of eight child, Darryl Sittler learned early on about responsibility. He would need all that inner strength and then some as captain of the Toronto Maple Leafs – and as an employee of notorious, cantankerous owner Harold Ballard.

"I was a pretty mature kid growing up," said Sittler, who still owns the Leafs' franchise records for goals and points (Mats Sundin is set to overtake both marks in 2007–08). "I had a good work ethic thanks to my family. Playing in Toronto was a challenge for a number of reasons, and I think having such a stable base at home made it much easier."

Toronto made Sittler the eighth overall pick in the 1970 draft. After two years of developing his talents and overcoming a broken wrist, Sittler blossomed in 1972–73, notching 48 assists and 77 points in 78 games for the Leafs.

The next year, he had 38 goals and 84 points, and Toronto made the playoffs for the first of eight straight seasons with Sittler in the lineup. And the year after that, when Dave Keon departed for the World Hockey Association, Sittler was given the *C*.

"Being captain of the Maple Leafs was never something I took lightly," he said. "I was very aware of what a prominent role you took on in that capacity. It was one of the biggest honors I ever had in the game."

Sittler elevated his play in his first season as captain, collecting 41 goals and his first 100-point campaign in 1975–76. He also scored five goals in a single playoff game against the Flyers that year, but his most noteworthy achievement came at Maple Leaf Gardens on Feb. 7, 1976, against Boston.

Darryl Sittler Fast Facts

NHL career:	1970–85
Teams:	Toronto, Philadelphia, Detroit
Post-expansion stats:	484 goals, 637 assists, 1,121 points in 1,096 games
Playoff stats:	29 goals, 45 assists, 74 points in 76 games
Individual awards:	None
First-team all-star berths:	0
Second-team all-star berths:	1 ('78)
Stanley Cups:	0
Legacy:	Maple Leafs legend set NHL record with 10-point game.

A one-man wrecking crew in an 11-4 rout of the Bruins, Sittler scored six goals and 10 points that night, setting an NHL record that has yet to be broken. And, as the game was televised on CBC's *Hockey Night In Canada*, it solidified him across the country as a bona fide superstar.

"I still have people come up and talk to me about that game," Sittler said. "You can never explain why that kind of thing happens to you. You're just thankful it did happen."

Sittler's star was still on the rise. He made Team Canada's roster for the inaugural Canada Cup in 1976, and, acting on a tip from assistant coach Don Cherry, scored the overtime winner in the game that clinched the tournament for the Canadians.

"No doubt, that's one of the highlights of my career," said Sittler, who streaked down the left wing, faked a shot on Czech goalie Vladimir Dzurilla, then skated around him and scored into an open net. "Scoring a goal in the NHL is one thing, but scoring for your country… The feeling is just out of this world."

Sittler's Leafs also were improving, upsetting the New York Islanders in the 1978 quarterfinal before being swept by Montreal in the semis. But by 1979–80, Ballard had brought back Punch Imlach to run the club. And the match between team brain trust and star player was not made in heaven.

> **"Scoring a goal in the NHL is one thing, but scoring for your country... The feeling is just out of this world."**
>
> **– Darryl Sittler**

One by one, Sittler's friends on Toronto's roster were dealt away. The cruelest blow came when his best friend on the team, Lanny McDonald, was shipped to Colorado in December of 1979. The tension between Sittler and the Ballard-Imlach duo increased to the point where Sittler removed the *C* from his jersey in a protest against the dismantling of what had been a promising team.

"It was a battle of wills," Sittler said. "Imlach wanted to break me down, and I wanted to stay and help the team play well. Saying it tested my resolve is probably an understatement. But initially, I thought I could still stay with Toronto. It just didn't work out that way."

Worn out and tired of battling Ballard, Sittler waived his no-trade clause and was dealt to Philadelphia midway through the 1981–82 campaign. He had 83 points and an all-star game appearance in his first full season with the Flyers but was shipped to Detroit in 1984 and retired after one year with the Red Wings.

"It wasn't the ideal way to end things," said Sittler, whose NHL totals include 484 goals and 1,121 points in 1,096 games. "But I still had an incredible career.

"So few people have the chance to experience the things that I've experienced in my life. There were times that weren't easy for me and my family, that's for sure. But the positives have far outweighed the negatives. And being fortunate enough to play in a city like Toronto, a place where hockey is so much a part of people's lives, you'd never trade that for anything."

– AP

59

Borje Salming

The Import

When Borje Salming arrived in North America to begin his NHL career, he was excited and concerned all at once.

"It is a dream to come here to play," he said, "but some warned me I would come back a cripple."

Indeed, in Salming's 17 years in the league, the hockey gods threw everything they had at the skillful, bullet-quick blueliner. During the course of his career, he endured a bruised chest, broken bones, a cracked heel, a charley horse and a deep facial laceration that required nearly 300 stitches, to name but a few of his serious injuries.

But Salming, called King by his teammates, emerged not only with a spot in the Hall of Fame, but also as a pioneer for all European players and a national hero in his native Sweden.

Born in the mining town of Kiruna, Salming grew up without his father, who died in a tragic accident. Aside from his brother, mother and two sisters, hockey was all he had.

"I started playing hockey at age seven and practised very hard at the game," said Salming in 1976. "It was all I wanted to do. I tried to be a good student in school, but I wasn't because most of the time I was too tired from playing the game.

"In time, I made the championship team in my country, but I still had to work as a machinist to make a living. That is why if I wanted hockey, I had to come [to the NHL]."

Salming was discovered by Leafs scout Gerry McNamara, who initially was sent over to look at goalie Kurt Larsson. McNamara returned to Toronto far more impressed with Salming and eventual Toronto teammate Inge Hammarstrom.

He was hyped as "the Bobby Orr of the Swedish major leagues," but when Salming joined the Leafs as a 22-year-old in 1973, he wasn't entirely certain he belonged in the NHL.

"You must remember, until the last few years bodychecking was not permitted in Sweden," he said. "I did not know if I could adjust to [the NHL] style, and did not know if I could make it."

Salming adjusted rather quickly – he was named the first star in his first-ever NHL game – and finished his rookie season in Toronto with a respectable 34 assists and 39 points in 76 games. His defense, though, was far more developed.

"He blocks shots better than almost anyone, and when he goes down, he bounces back up faster than others do," said Leafs coach Red Kelly at the time. "He uses his stick skillfully. He uses his feet like another stick. He doesn't hit a lot, but he doesn't have to. He has a lot of little tricks up his sleeve."

As one of the most prominent members of the so-called European invasion, Salming was subjected to ugly taunts from xenophobic fans and players. He heard them when they called him a "chicken Swede" in the early years, but ultimately Salming earned the respect of the entire hockey world.

> **"There's just no player who does as many things as Borje does."**
>
> **– Lanny McDonald**

"There's just no player who does as many things as Borje does," said Lanny McDonald in 1977. "There isn't a player in the NHL who's as valuable to his team as Salming is to us."

Because he played in an era where the Maple Leafs were more of a sideshow than Stanley Cup contender, Salming skated in only 81 playoff games. However, his consistency at both ends of the rink – he had at least 40 assists and 56 points in seven consecutive seasons – and the 30-plus minutes he played each game made Salming a legend in Leafland, as well as in his homeland.

For Salming, it was easier to deal with the physical pain than it was watching the Leafs tread water or sink year after year.

"Sometimes you have years where you are going to get hurt," said Salming, a two-time runner-up for the Norris Trophy. "You've just got to accept it, there's nothing you can do. It is frustrating, though, when the team is losing and you're not in the lineup to try and help."

In 1986, Salming found himself in the media spotlight for the wrong reasons.

After a *Sports Illustrated* story alleged members of the Edmonton Oilers were involved in illegal drug use, Salming told the *Toronto Star* that he had experimented with cocaine five years earlier. The league initially suspended him for the entire '86–87 campaign, but he was reinstated after eight games.

"I was the only one to come forward about it, so I was the one example," Salming said. "I have no regrets, and I have nothing against [NHL president] John Ziegler."

Salming left the Leafs after 16 seasons and spent the last year of his NHL career with Detroit in 1989–90. He played two-plus seasons in Sweden after that before hanging up his skates for good in 1993.

The Hall of Fame came calling in 1996, making Salming its first-ever Swedish member. It was no faint praise for a superstar who forged the way with his tough-but-classy style of play.

"I do not believe I have to be the goon to play well," Salming once said. "I play hard, but not to hurt. I will not back down, but I do not look for the fight. I do everything I can to help my team win."

– AP

Borje Salming Fast Facts

NHL career:	1973–90
Teams:	Toronto, Detroit
Post-expansion stats:	150 goals, 637 assists, 787 points in 1,148 games
Playoff stats:	12 goals, 37 assists, 49 points in 81 games
Individual awards:	None
First-team all-star berths:	1 ('77)
Second-team all-star berths:	5 ('75, '76, '78, '79, '80)
Stanley Cups:	0
Legacy:	Swedish native the league's first European-born superstar.

Sergei Fedorov

Mr. Do-it-all

On the ice or off it, Sergei Fedorov made things happen. He left his communist homeland for the freedom offered by a life in hockey. He married a world-famous tennis player. He could play any position except for goalie, and play it superbly. And for the better part of a decade, he was instrumental in the Detroit Red Wings' hockey dominance.

"Everybody thinks of me as a skater, going fast, making quick decisions with the puck, going 100 miles an hour," said Fedorov, a three-time Stanley Cup champion with Detroit. "But I'm very proud that I played at both ends of the ice and that I learned what it takes to come together as part of a team and achieve unbelievable goals."

One of the first prominent Russians to defect to North America, Fedorov joined the Red Wings barely out of his teens. Unfamiliar with the language and far from home, he managed to not skip a beat on the ice – scoring 31 goals and 79 points in his rookie season of 1990–91 – but his adjustments away from the arena weren't nearly as easy.

"On the ice, it was exciting as can be, playing in front of 20,000 people every night," he said. "I wasn't very experienced in life when I came over, and not being able to be with your friends and your relatives was tough in the beginning. Very tough. I just got lucky that I ran into people who really care about me and helped me through a lot of off-ice things."

Fedorov improved his goal and point totals in both his sophomore and third NHL seasons. Then, he exploded for 56 goals and 120 points in '93–94; even more impressively, he also won the Hart Trophy as league MVP and Selke Trophy as best defensive forward – a feat that hasn't been matched before or since.

"I played a lot of minutes that particular season and really got the chance to test my limits," Fedorov said. "When you're really focused in that way, you can see the play maybe a second slower. It was an unbelievable time."

Fedorov averaged more than a point per game in each of the next two seasons, but his ice time and offensive numbers fell off in '96–97. Although confused by the changes at first, he eventually learned the most crucial lesson that any player ever learns.

"I was frustrated, because I thought [the 120-point season] should be my limitation, if you will," he said. "My minutes were cut pretty well… I wasn't playing 27, 28; it was 20 or 21 minutes, and I didn't understand enough until I looked into it and talked to some veteran players and my friends.

"I didn't realize we had a pretty good team and we were trying to achieve a team goal, which was winning the Stanley Cup. That was part of growing up and learning."

The lesson paid the biggest of hockey dividends that same year, as he won his first championship.

> "I'm very proud that I played at both ends of the ice and that I learned what it takes to come together as part of a team and achieve unbelievable goals."
>
> – Sergei Fedorov

"Once you get there, you feel like you've climbed over Mt. Everest," said Fedorov, who experienced the same sensation again in 1998 when the Wings repeated as champs. "But in reality, you just did your job much better, you were more focused, you were more experienced, you played the game all-out for 60 minutes… all those things you hear every night from the coaches."

After a messy contract dispute that saw Fedorov sign with the Carolina Hurricanes in 1997 before Detroit matched the offer, the Russian remained in Motown and won his third Cup in 2002. (In a subsequent interview with *The Hockey News*, he revealed he'd been secretly married to tennis star Anna Kournikova from 2001 to 2003.)

However, a year after his final Cup win in Detroit, he and Wings management couldn't see eye-to-eye on a new deal, and he signed with Anaheim in 2003.

"I've always had tough contract negotiations," he said. "Maybe it's my agents, maybe it's me, maybe it's the other party that's involved, who knows. But I've always seemed to have a hard time.

"At the end, it didn't happen for me in Detroit the way I thought I deserved. I was in turmoil with my private life, couldn't think straight and didn't get professional support from my agents. It just wasn't the best time for me or Detroit. And I moved on."

Fedorov lasted a little more than a year with the Mighty Ducks before he was dealt to Columbus in 2005.

"It was exciting, because [Blue Jackets GM] Doug MacLean knew me since I was 20 years old in Detroit, and I played with [Jackets coach] Gerard Gallant there," Fedorov said. "It was a good environment to come in, it had a different focus, and it was closer to my home in Detroit."

Fedorov's individual and team successes prove that, contrary to Don Cherry's insinuations, players from Russia or any part of Europe can conjure up the requisite heart and grit to claim a Cup.

"[Cherry] maybe was right about us not knowing [what it took to win], but how could we know?" Fedorov said. "We had to learn how to get there like everybody else, to lose a few times and learn what it took to win. It's a rough, bloody, bumpy and very painful road."

– AP

Sergei Fedorov Fast Facts

NHL career:	1990–2007 (active)
Teams:	Detroit, Anaheim, Columbus
Post-expansion stats:	461 goals, 644 assists, 1,105 points in 1,128 games
Playoff stats:	50 goals, 113 assists, 163 points in 162 games
Individual awards:	
• Hart Trophy	('94)
• Selke Trophy	('94, '96)
First-team all-star berths:	1 ('94)
Second-team all-star berths:	0
Stanley Cups:	2
Legacy:	Versatile Russian only player in league history to win Hart and Selke in same season.

The next 10

Now that you've come to the end of the book, you may be wondering which young players are good bets to make the cut the next time *The Hockey News* compiles an all-time list of the NHL's greatest players.

Well, wonder no more. After consulting a number of veteran observers at the pro and amateur levels, we've put together a list of 10 players who could be headlining our next project.

In alphabetical order, here are 10 young NHLers to watch:

Rick DiPietro, G (New York Islanders): Some thought Isles' owner Charles Wang should've had his franchise revoked for signing the team's 25-year-old goaltender to a 15-year, $67.5-million contract in 2006. But if anyone can fulfill the expectations that come with such a contract, it's DiPietro, the first goalie ever selected as the No. 1 pick in the NHL entry draft.

The Winthrop, Mass., native developed slowly after the Islanders chose him in 2000. He turned the corner in 2003–04, putting up his first winning record (23-18-5) and dropping his goals-against average from 2.97 to 2.36. And in 2006–07, he tied a franchise record for single-season wins (32), while posting the best save percentage (.919) of his NHL career.

"He's no kid anymore… the clock is ticking on him," said one scout of DiPietro. "Nevertheless, he's got all the tools and the mental makeup you look for in a consistently great, championship-caliber goalie. I still wouldn't have given him a 15-year contract, but I probably would've given him 10. To me, he's a no-doubter."

Marian Gaborik, RW (Minnesota): The key for Gaborik is his health. When he's got it, there are few players more talented with the puck than the Slovakian winger.

Although groin woes limited him to 48 regular season games with the Wild in 2006–07, he averaged 1.18 points per game – easily the best of his six-year career – and scored 30 goals.

"Let's be honest, Gaborik still has to prove himself in the playoffs," said one NHL GM. "In the regular season, though, there's no doubt he's one of the most dangerous players in the entire game."

Erik Johnson, D (St. Louis): The first pick in the 2006 NHL draft, Johnson possesses the size (6 foot 4) and mobility to star on the St. Louis blueline for 15 or 20 years. His passing and skating abilities are exquisite; he'll likely play major minutes in Missouri during his rookie NHL campaign – and by the end of it, he'll only be 20 years old.

"Imagine a faster Borje Salming," said one former NHL GM of Johnson. "There's no real weakness to his game at all. Some guys you just know are going to be great before they ever play a game in the NHL, and he's one of them."

Henrik Lundqvist, G (New York Rangers): Sweden isn't exactly known for its goal-tenders, but Lundqvist is in the process of changing all that.

"He can have an off-night every now and then," said one NHL scout of the Rangers' goalie. "But eight, eight-and-a-half times out of 10, he's one of the best players on the ice."

Lundqvist was named a finalist for the 2005–06 Vezina Trophy during his rookie season, won a gold medal for Sweden at the 2006 Olympics and earned 37 wins in his sophomore year.

"Playing well in the biggest market on earth can certainly raise your profile," said one GM. "Lundqvist is starting to become a legend there already."

Roberto Luongo, G (Vancouver): It took him seven years to play his first NHL post-season game, but in starring for the Canucks throughout 2006–07, Luongo has proven himself worthy of the hype.

"Steal of the century," said an anonymous NHL executive of the trade that sent Luongo to Vancouver in a multi-player deal. "Luongo is going to win Vezinas out west and probably some [Stanley] cups too."

Luongo, who has improved his win total in every NHL season – and won 47 for the Canucks in '06–07 – is as close to technically perfect as they come. And at age 28, his best years are still to come.

Alexander Ovechkin, LW (Washington): One of Russia's newest gifts to the NHL is also one of the league's most effervescent personalities. Which makes the fact that the 2006 Calder Trophy winner can back up his boasts on the ice much easier to take.

"Ovechkin is a cocky kid, but he's a good kid," said an NHL scout of the Capitals' star winger, who had 52 goals and 106 points in 2005–06 and then 46 goals and 92 points as a sophomore. "His defense isn't at an elite level, and in some respects he took a step back (in 2006–07), but he's still learning. Once he's finished, the world's his oyster."

Ovechkin already has scored one of the most famous goals in league history – while falling to the ice at Phoenix in January 2006 – and there's little doubt he'll be knocking home many more.

"The best Russian ever?" the scout said. "Could be. It's up to him."

Zach Parise, C (New Jersey): As he demonstrated in a major way during the 2007 playoffs, Parise has the speed, skill and grit to be an impact player.

Generously listed at 5 foot 11, he doesn't have much in the size department, but that never stopped his father, J-P Parise, from playing nearly 900 NHL games. And by his sophomore campaign with the Devils, Zach had already topped his father for goals in a single season (31).

"Oh, he'll be better than his dad," said a former NHL GM of the younger Parise. "Playing in New Jersey, he may not have many 100-plus point seasons, but he'll be the star there for as long as [Devils' GM] Lou [Lamoriello] can hold on to him."

Dion Phaneuf, D (Calgary): After just two seasons in the NHL, they're already making room for Phaneuf's name on the Norris Trophy as the league's best defenseman. The Edmonton native broke Gary Suter's franchise record in Calgary for goals by a rookie, and, late in his first year, Phaneuf became just the third rookie D-man in league history to crack the 20-goal plateau.

And just think – we haven't even mentioned yet how hard the guy hits.

"What's he got? What doesn't he have?" said one NHL GM. "He's ferocious, merciless on the ice. Ice water for blood. When his offense catches up to his defense, look out."

John Tavares, C (Oshawa, OHL): So many young players get tagged as The Next Wayne Gretzky, but Tavares already has done something that makes him worth comparing to the game's greatest player.

In 2006–07, at just 16 years of age, Tavares scored 72 goals in 67 games for the OHL's Oshawa Generals. In doing so, he broke Gretzky's OHL record of 70 goals in 64 games. And he won't be eligible for the NHL draft until 2009.

"He isn't going to steamroll over guys, but his hockey sense is already off the charts," said an amateur scout of Tavares. "Nobody knows what this kid's upper limits are yet. That's scary."

Jonathan Toews, C (Chicago): Selected third overall by the Blackhawks in the 2006 entry draft, Toews scored 22 goals and 39 points in 42 games with the University of North Dakota in 2006–07.

But he really made a name for himself at the 2007 world junior championship. In Canada's semifinal game against Team USA, the Winnipeg native scored on each of his three shootout opportunities to give the Canadians a 3-2 win. And Toews was the only non-NHLer on Canada's gold medal-winning entry at the '07 world championship in Moscow.

"Toews reminds me in some ways of Joey Nieuwendyk," said one NHL executive. "He can skate, he can distribute the puck. And the way he performed in that pressure-type situation [during the world junior championship]? That's vintage Nieuwendyk."